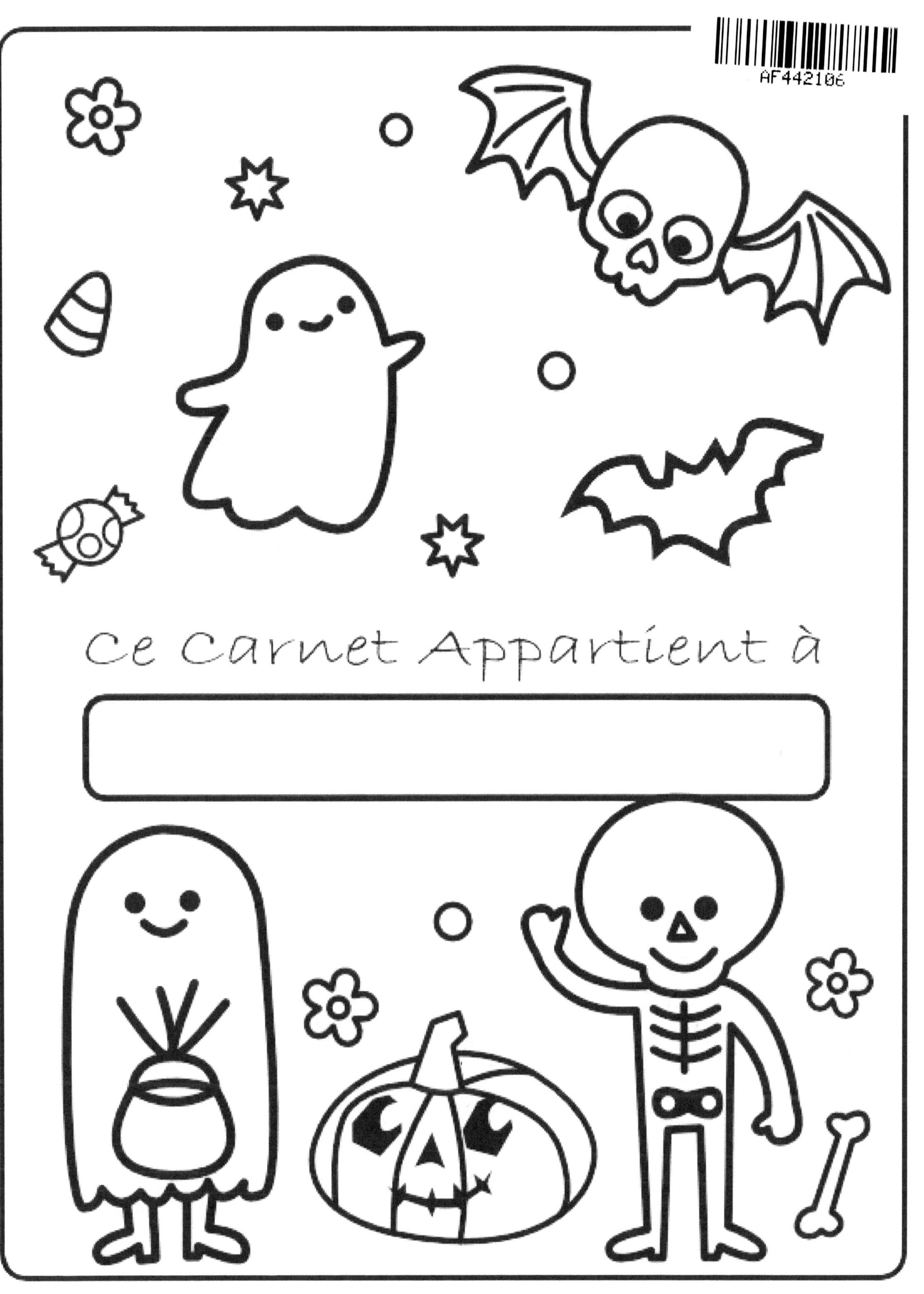

ce Carnet Appartient à

HALLOWEEN

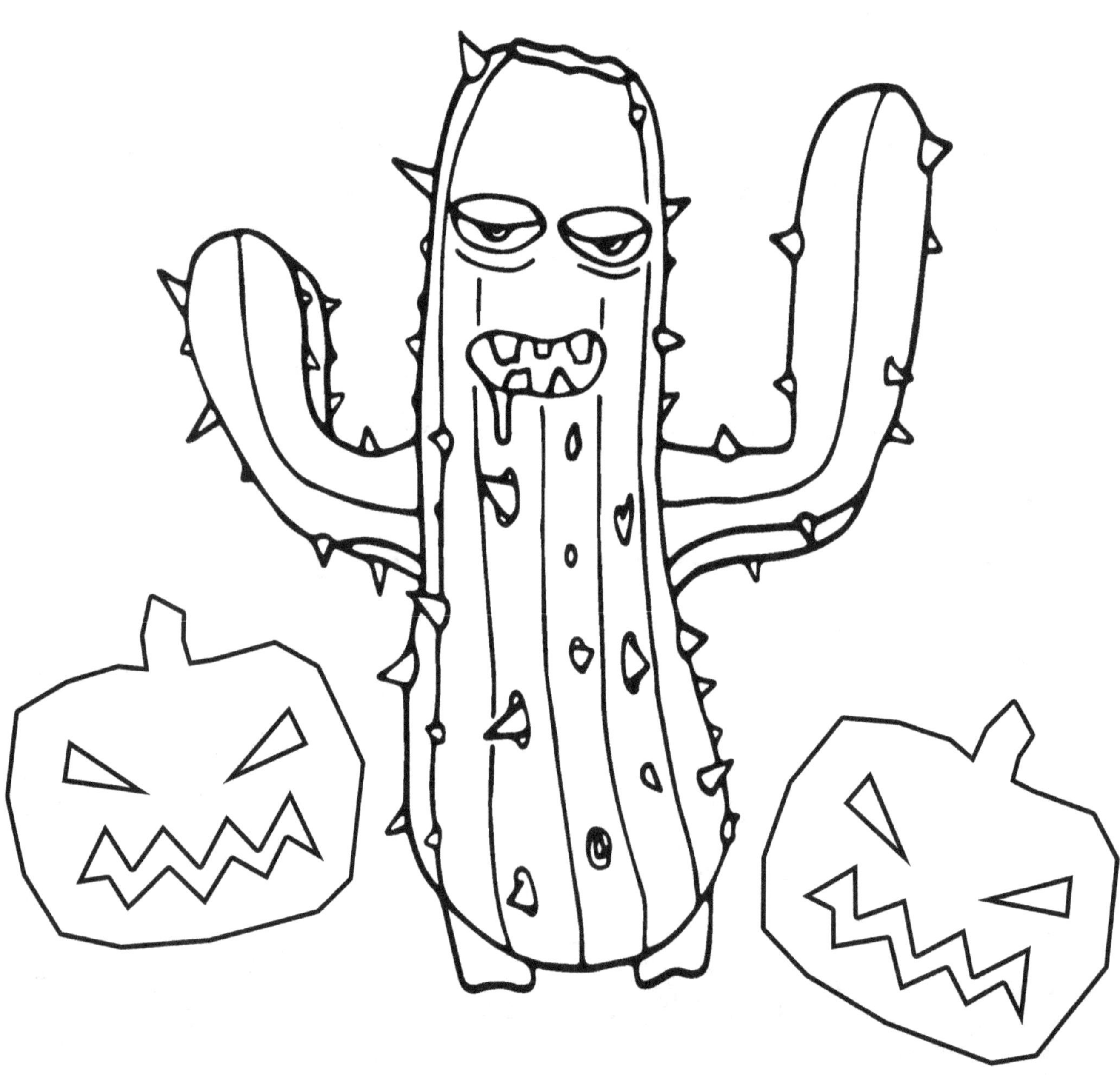

HALLOWEEN

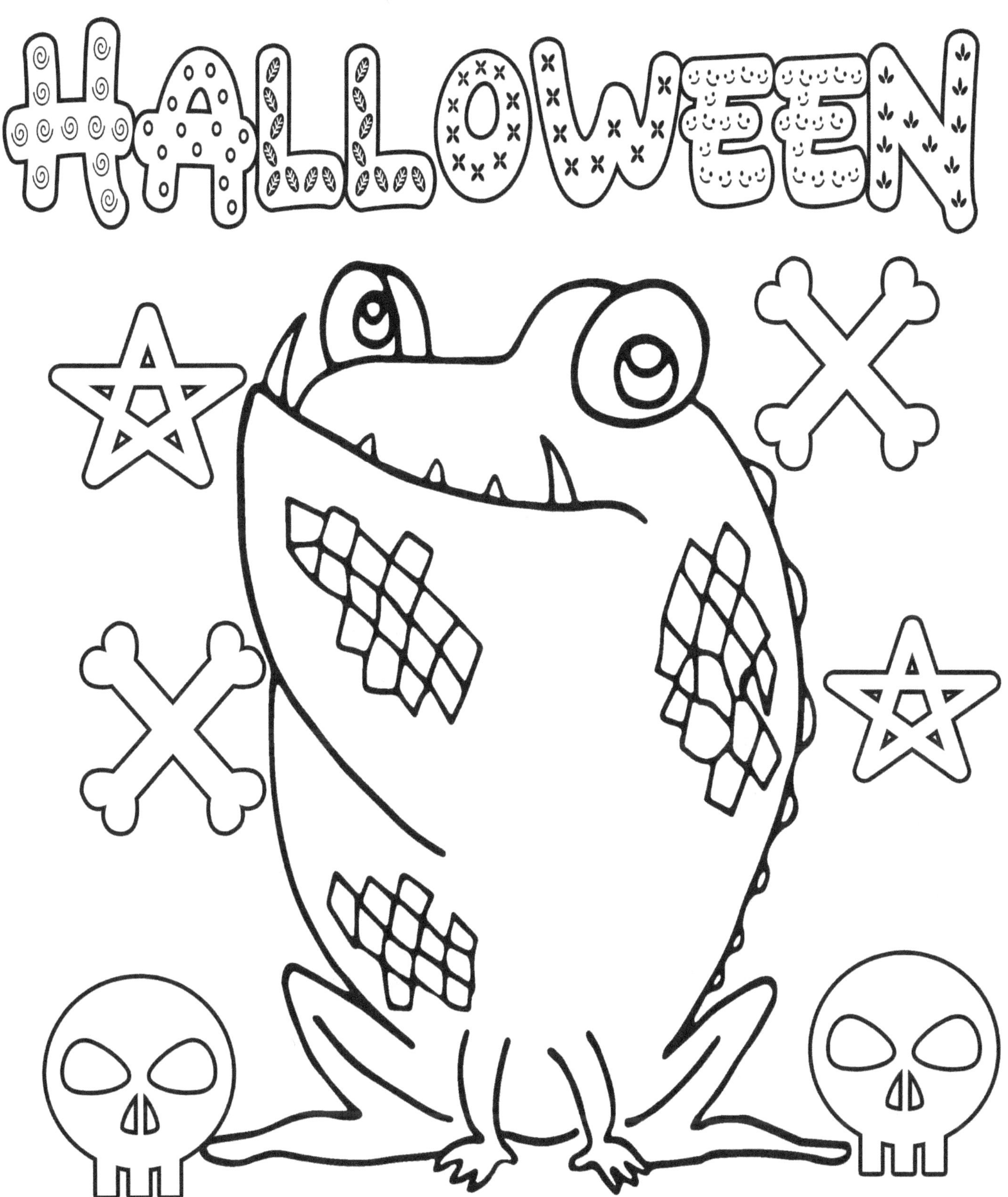

SPOOKY

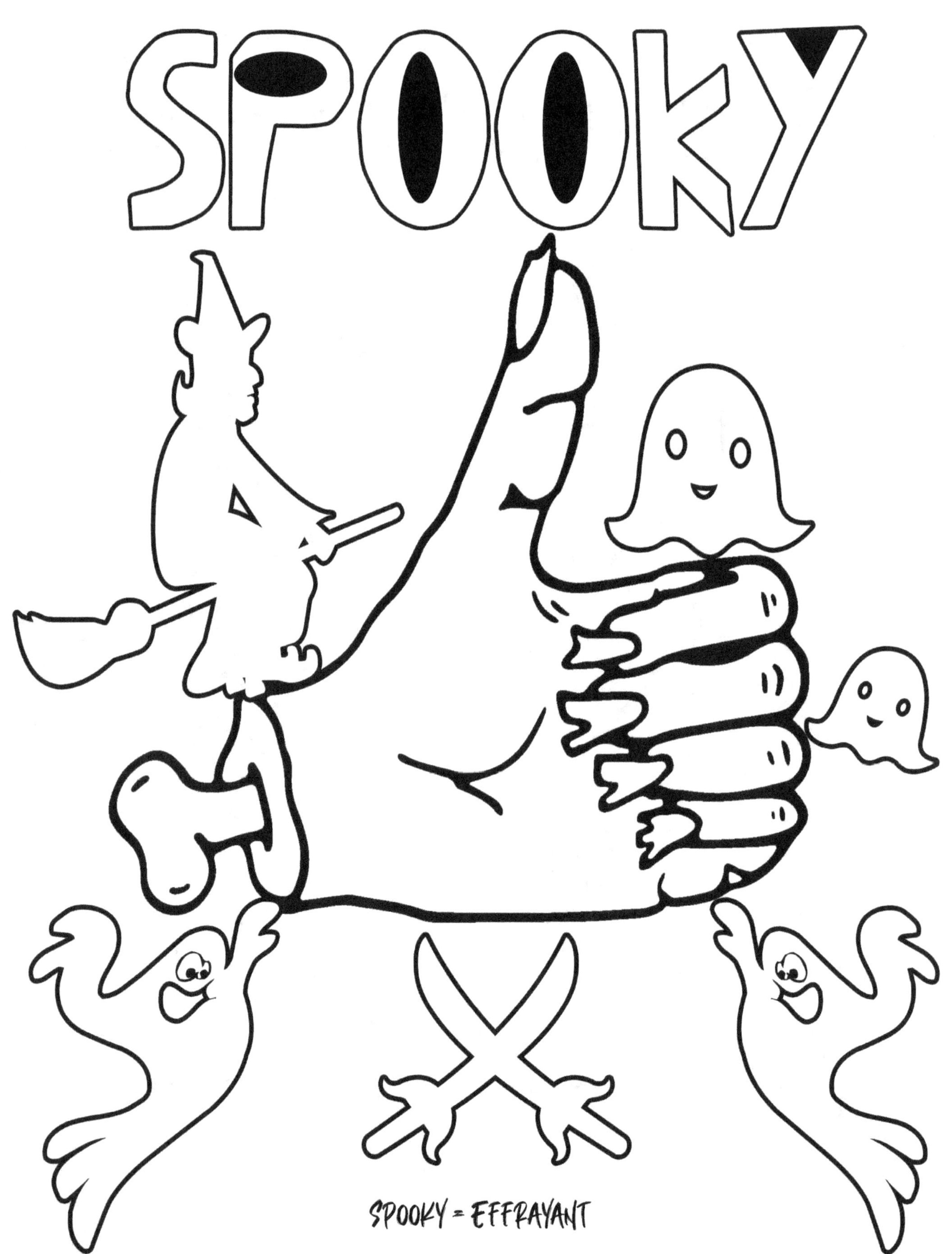

SPOOKY

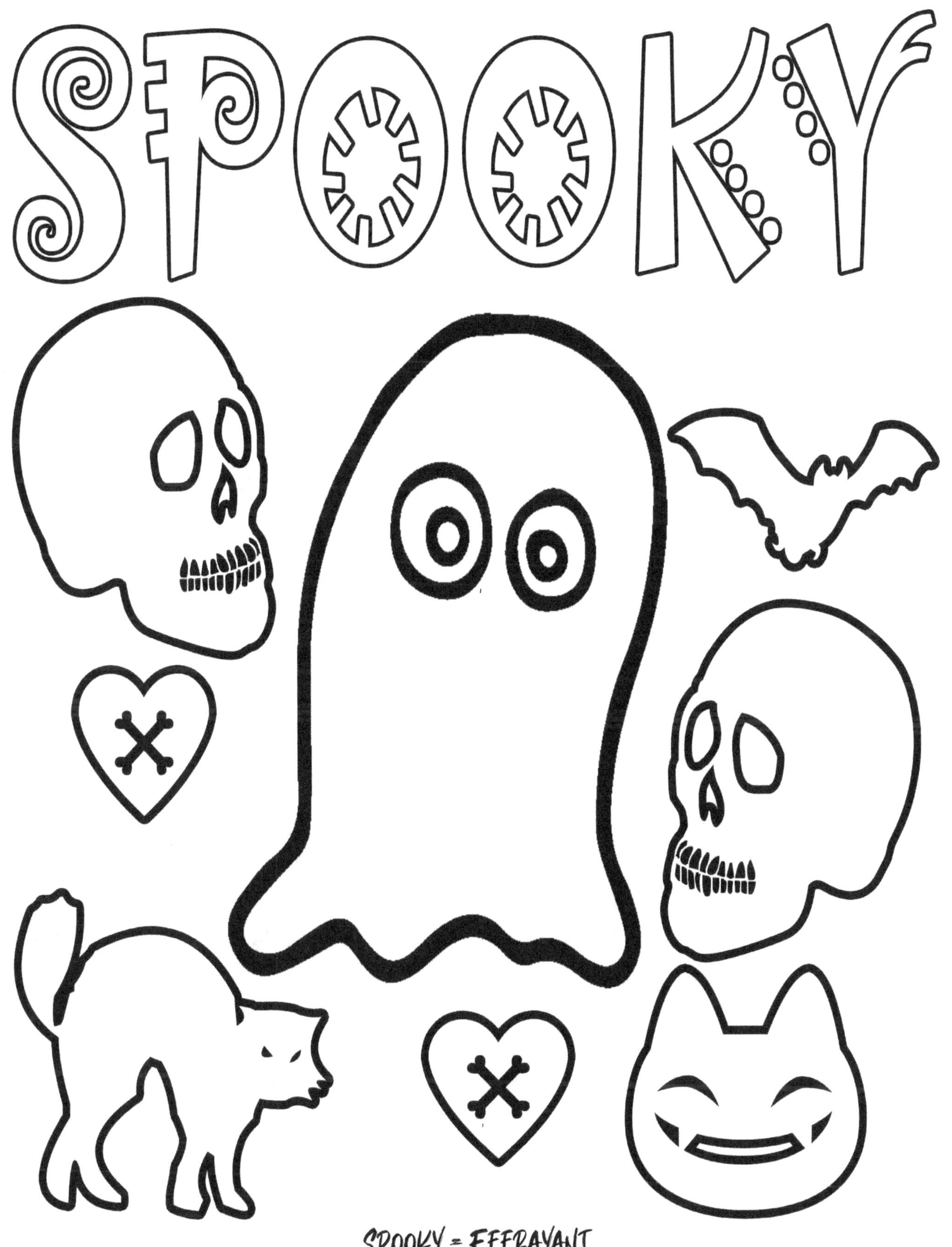

SPOOKY = EFFRAYANT

HORROR

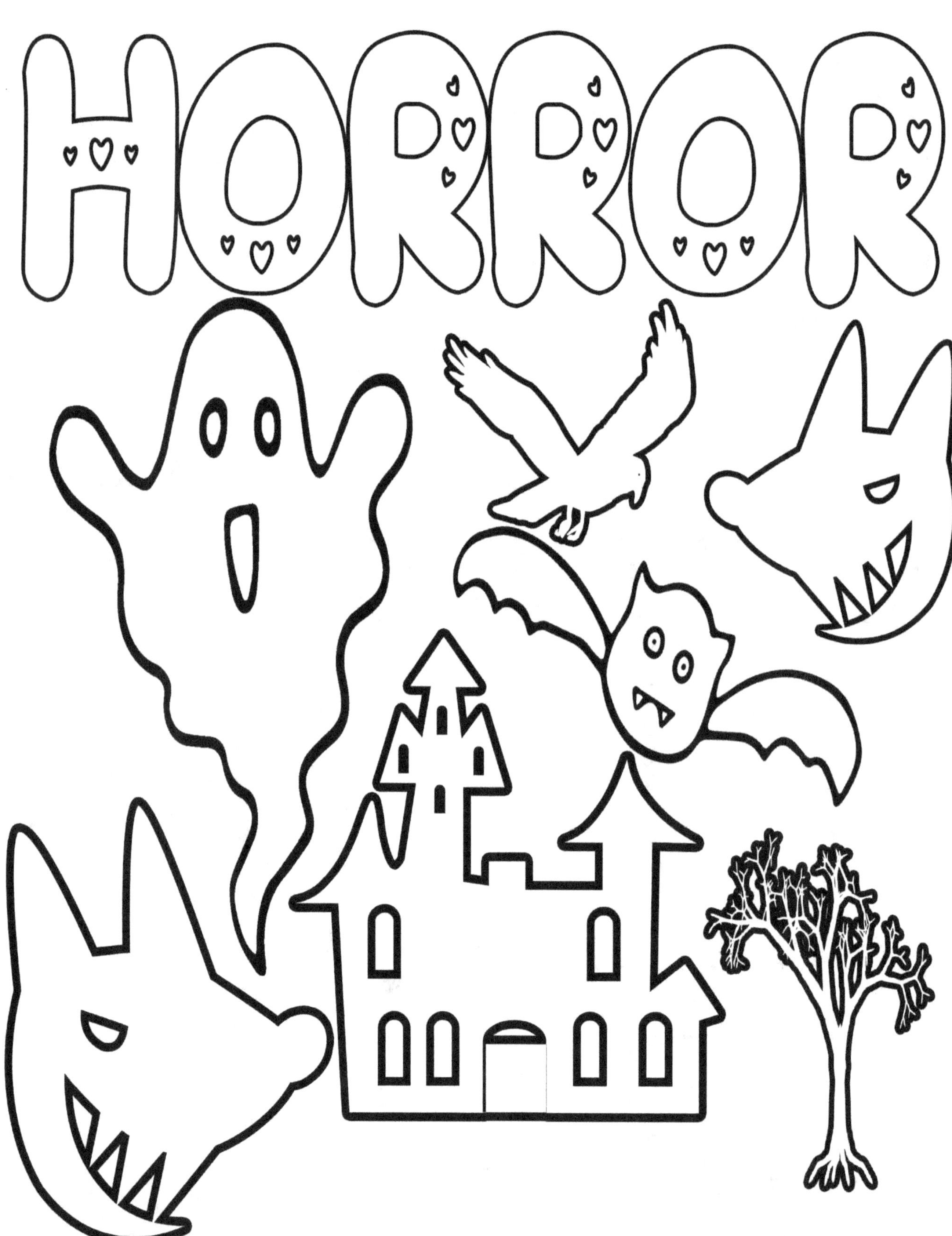

HORROR

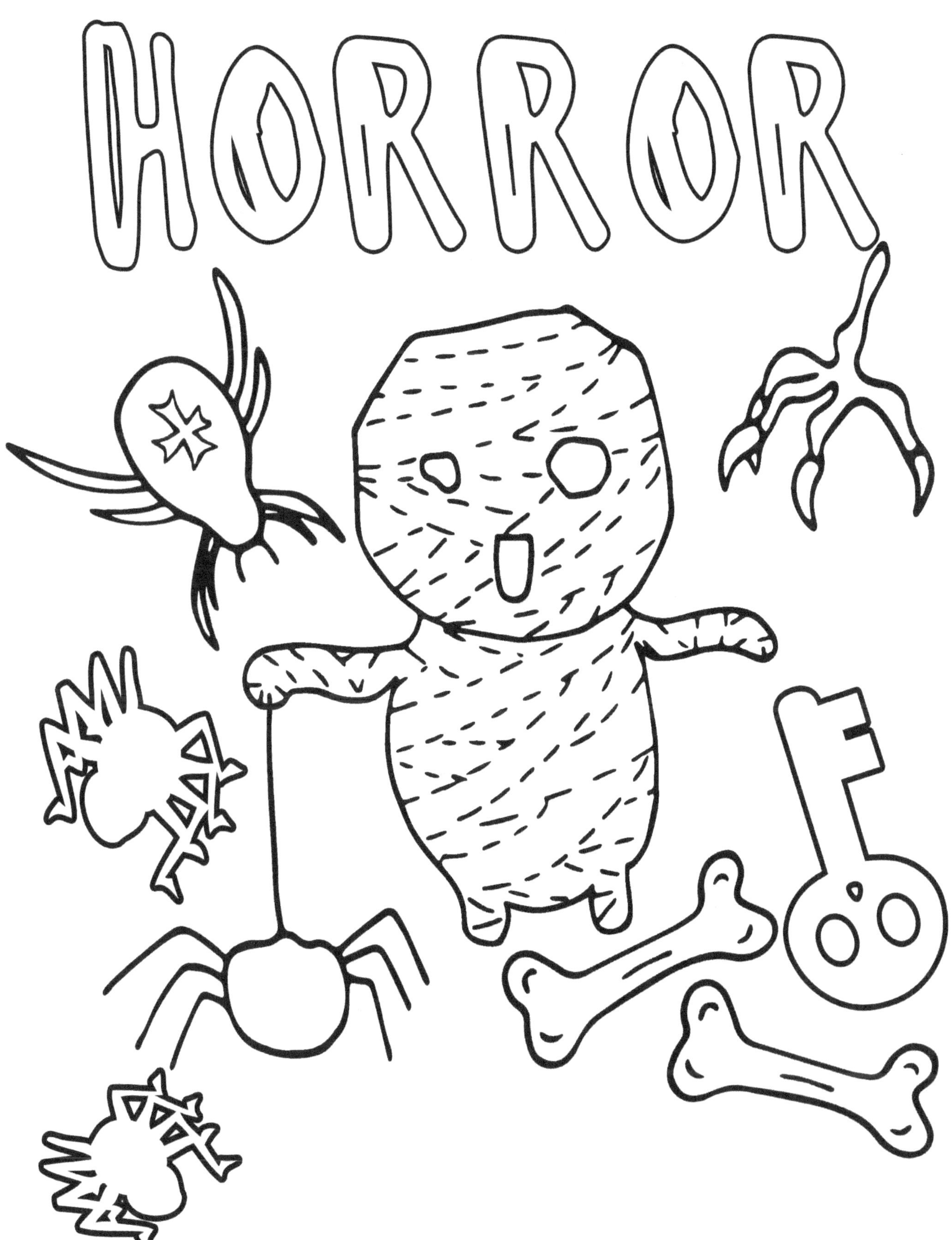

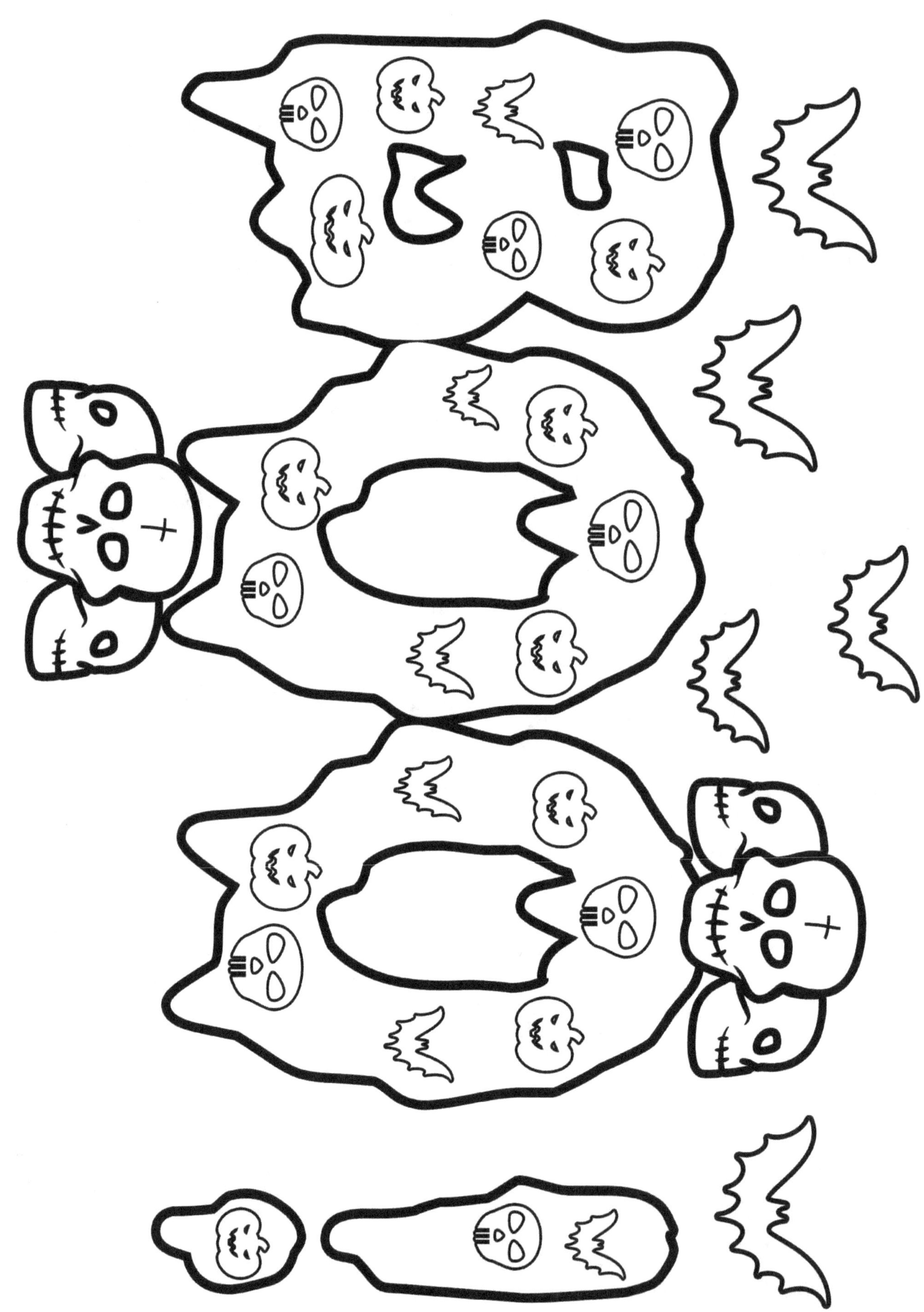

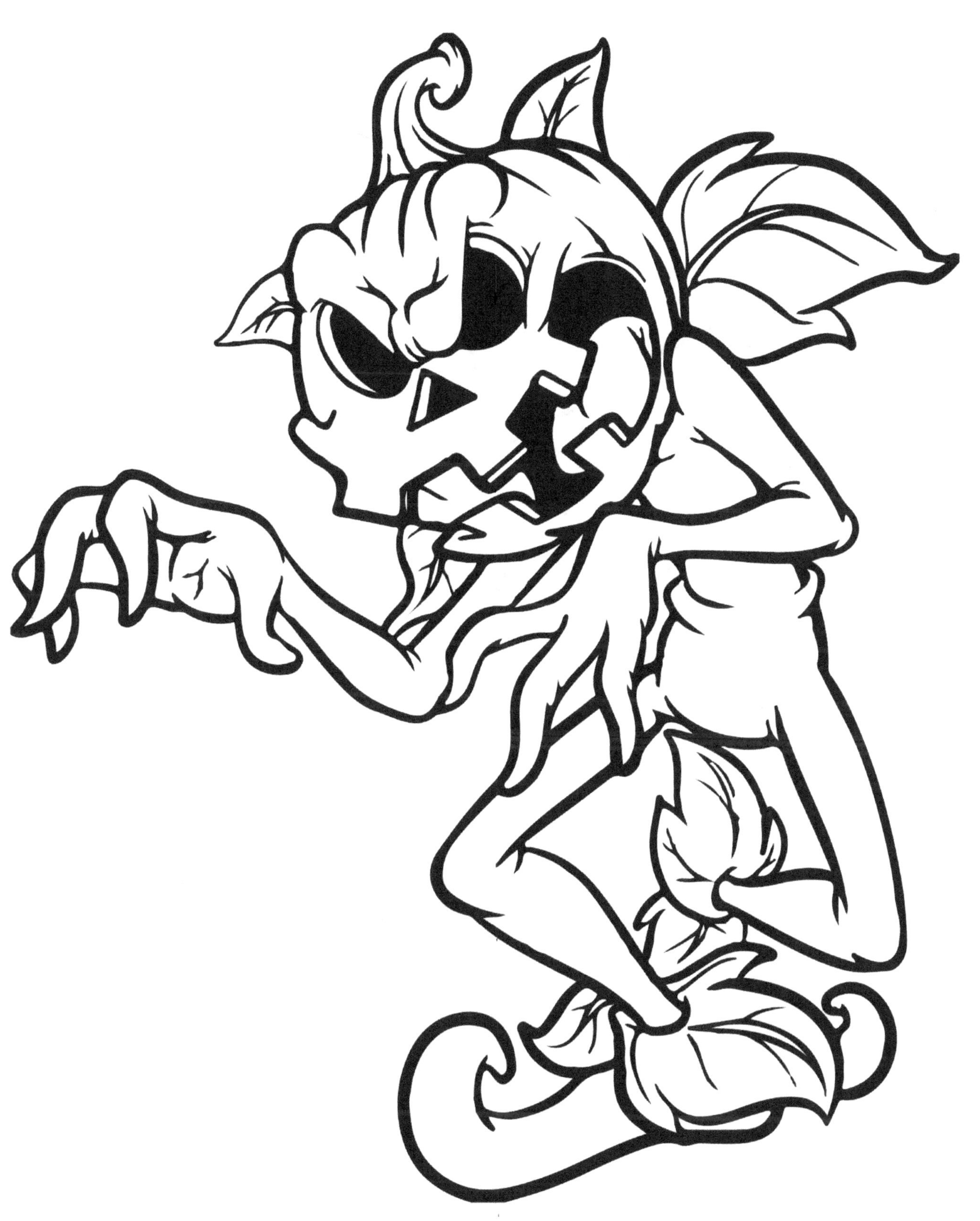

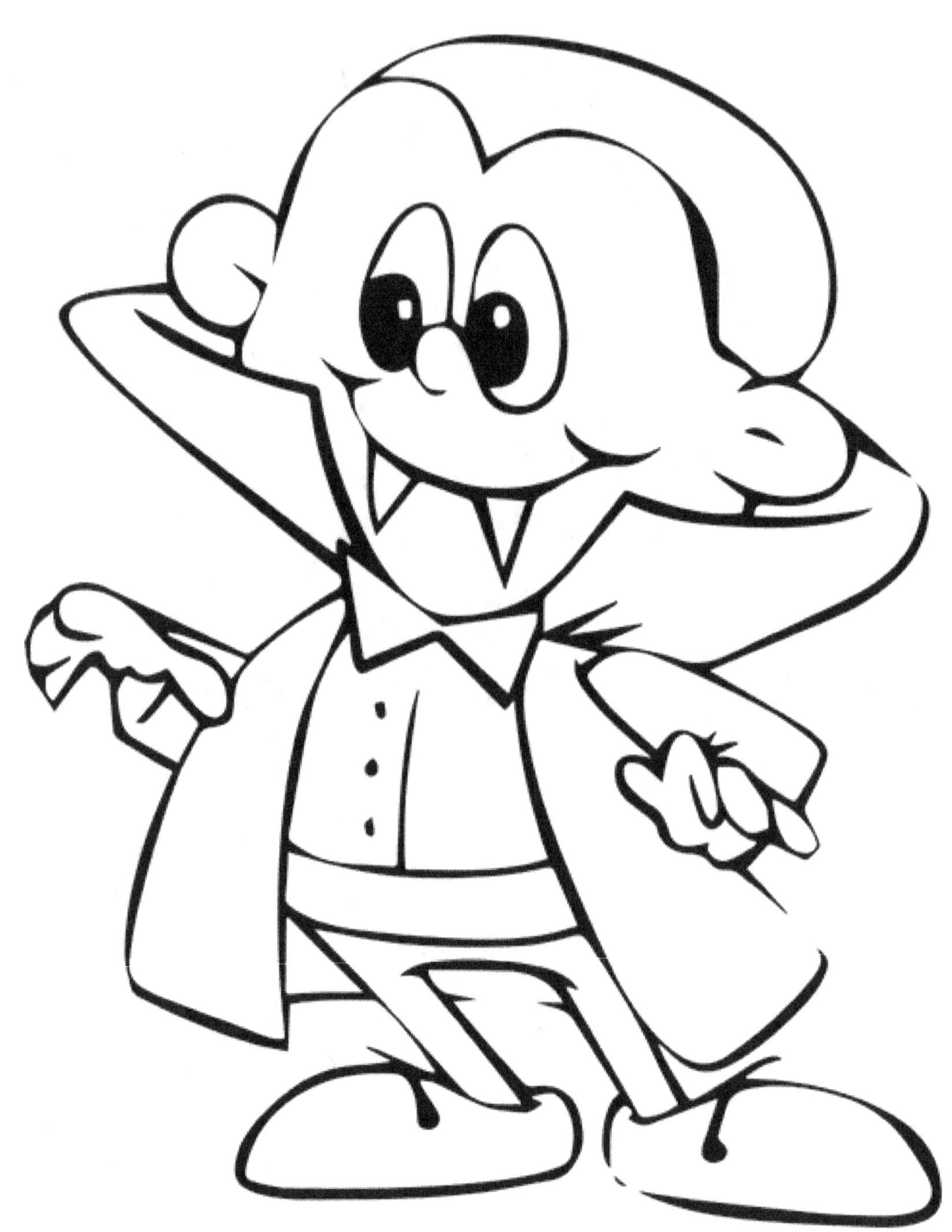

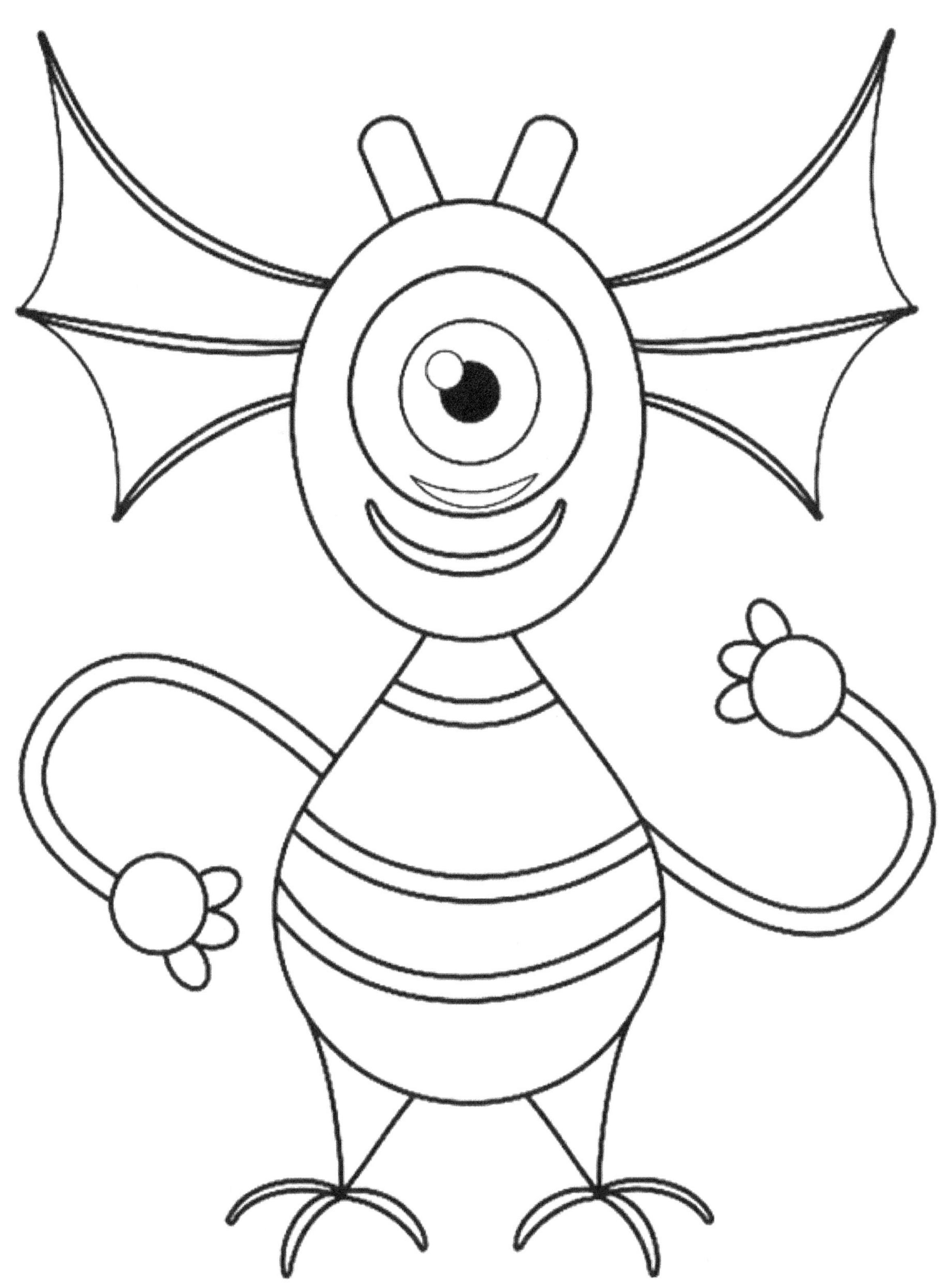

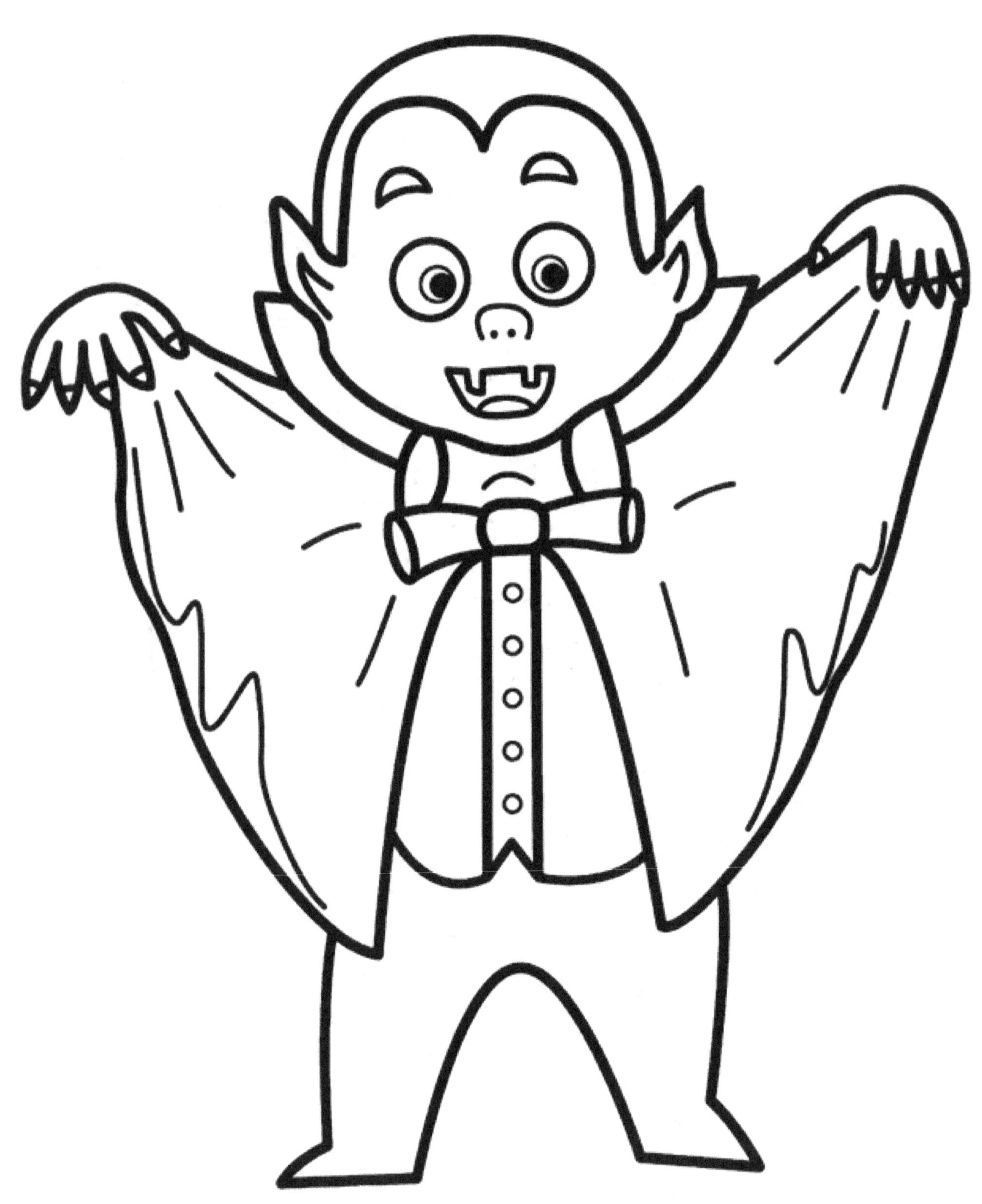

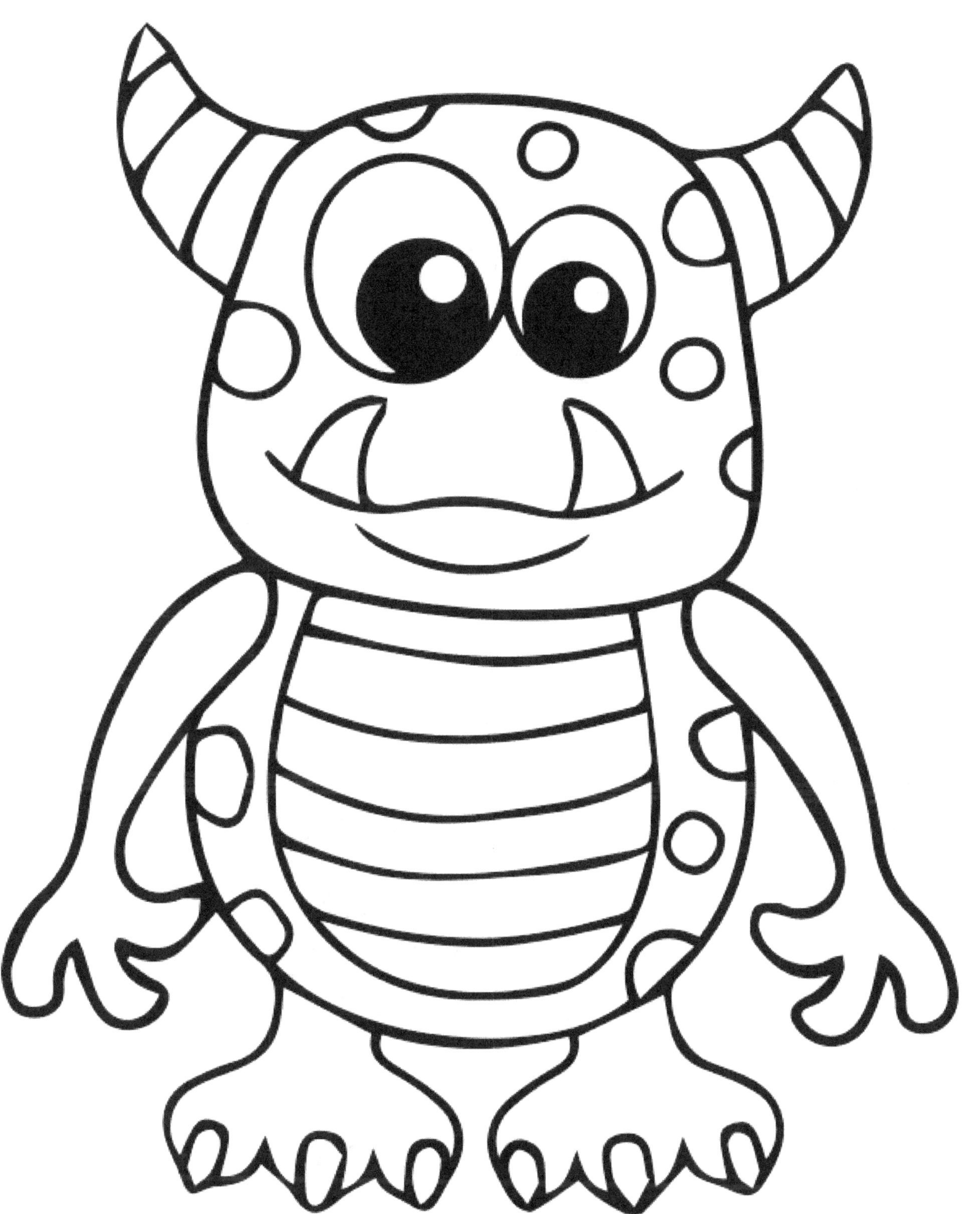

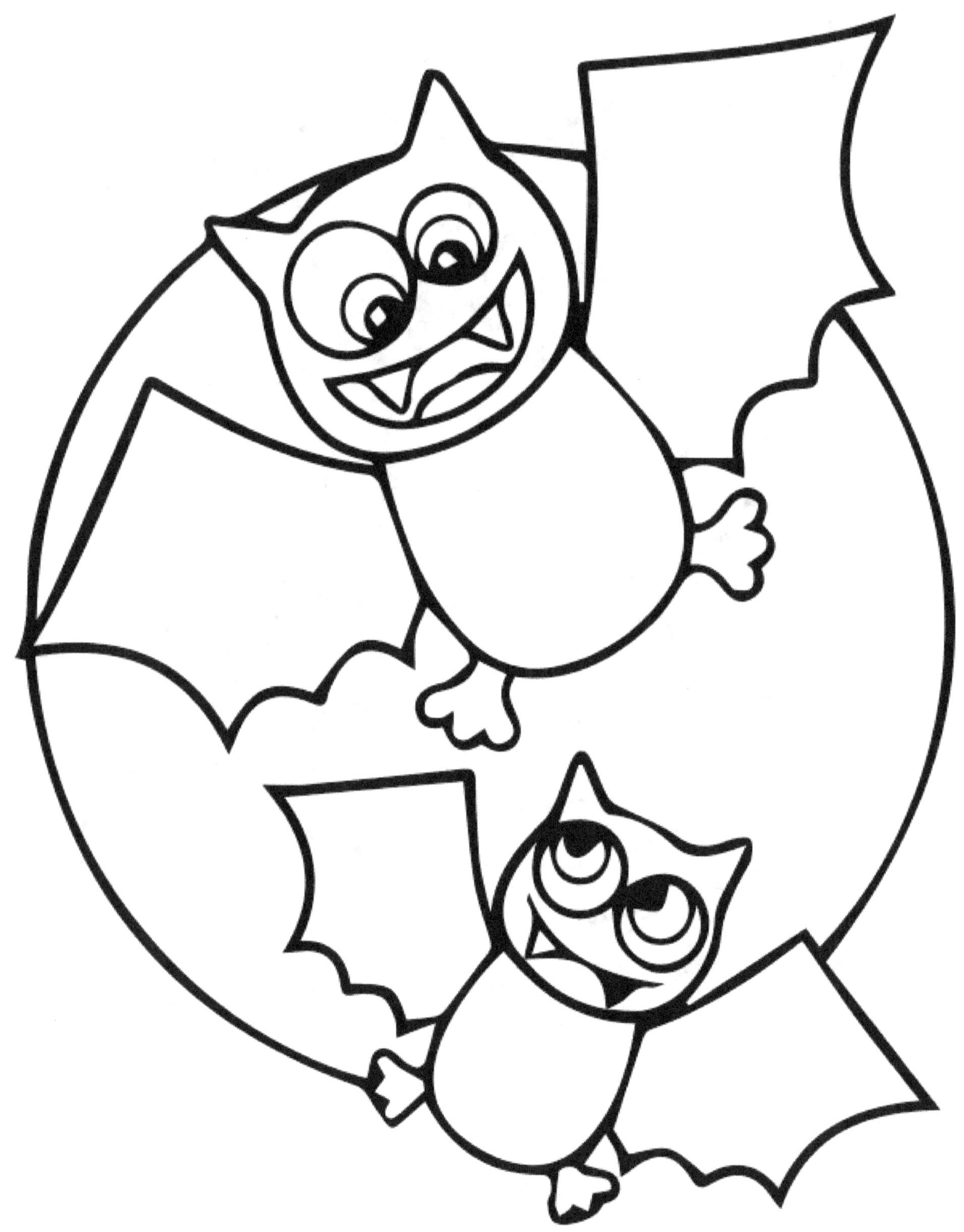

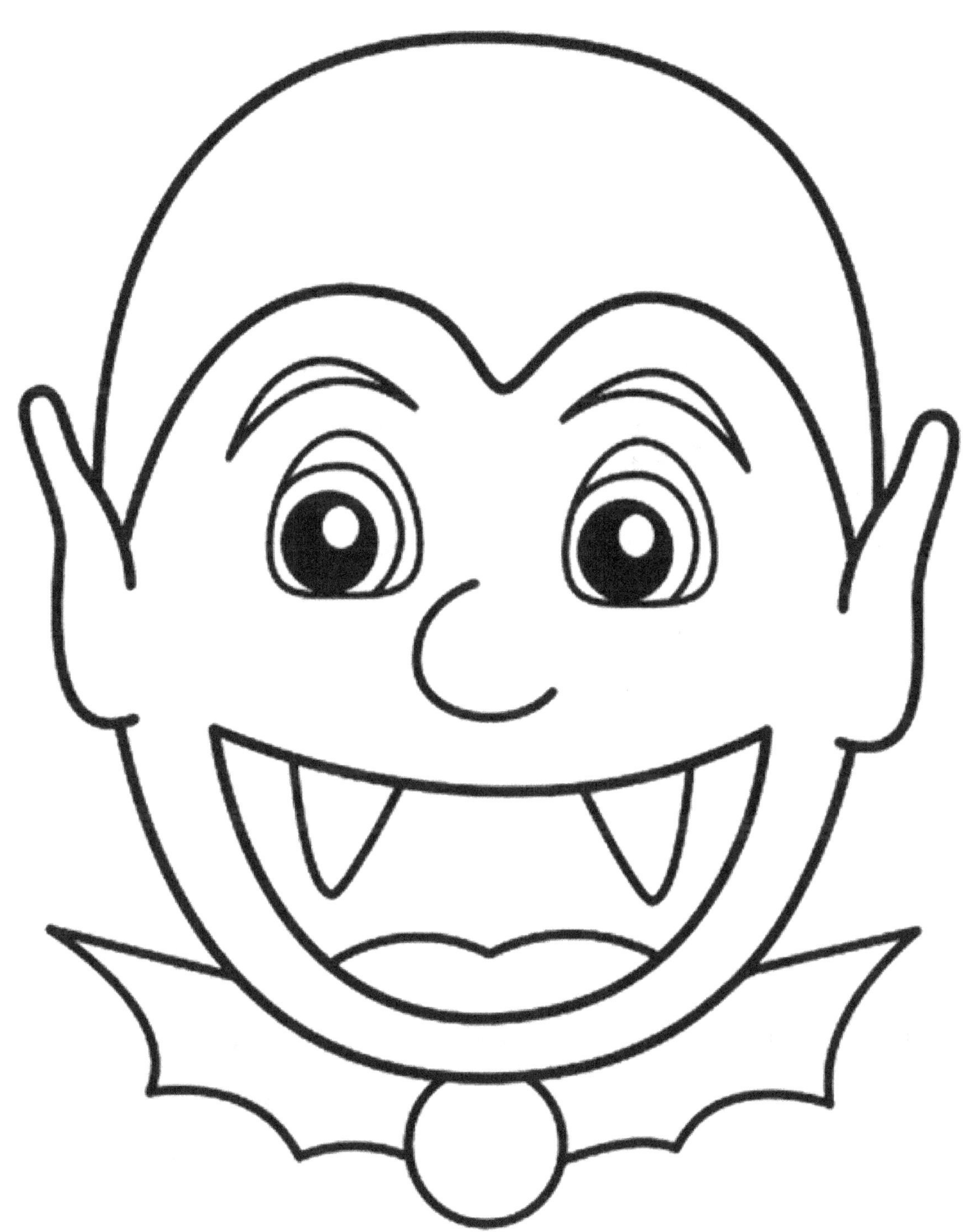

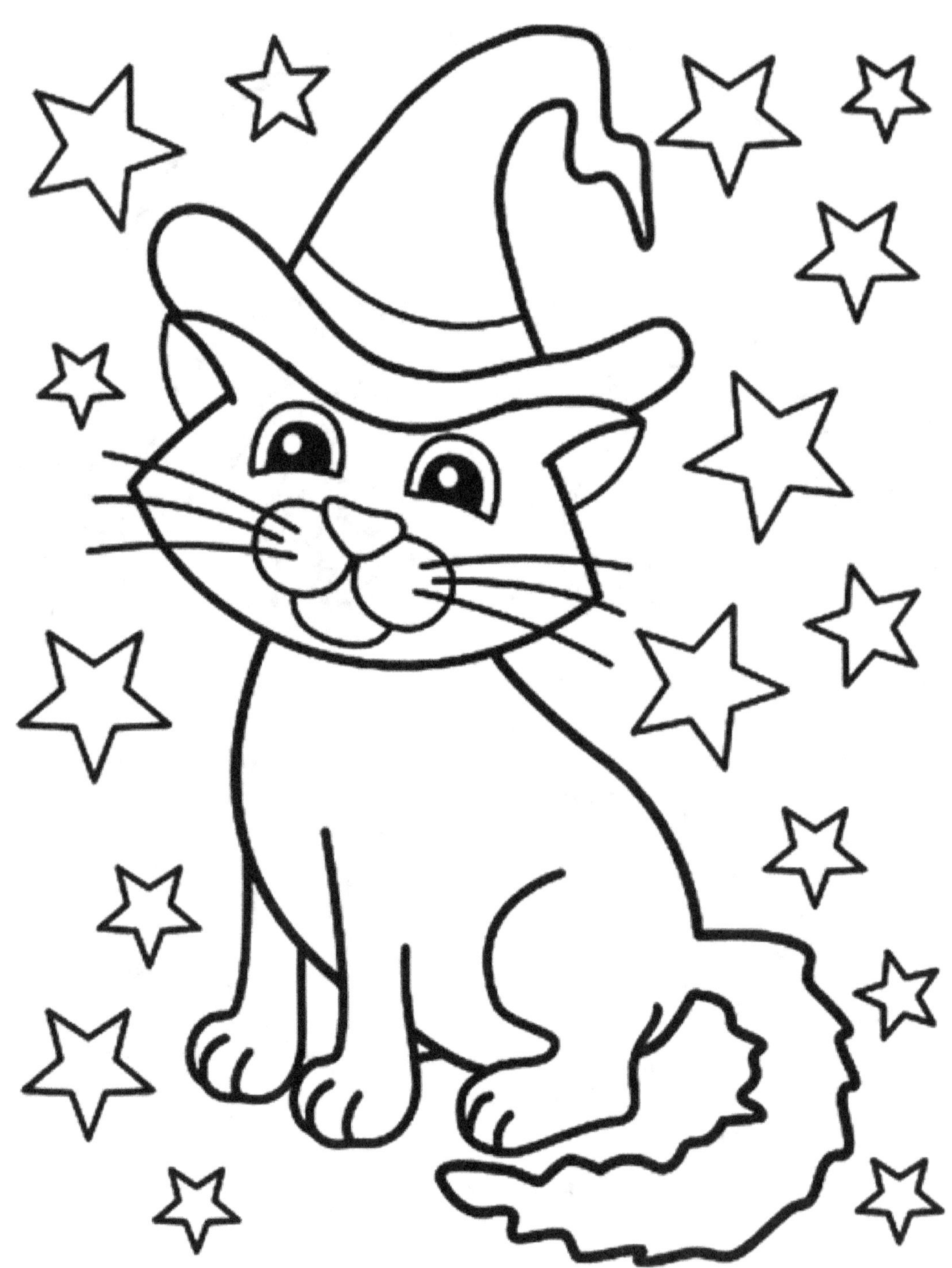

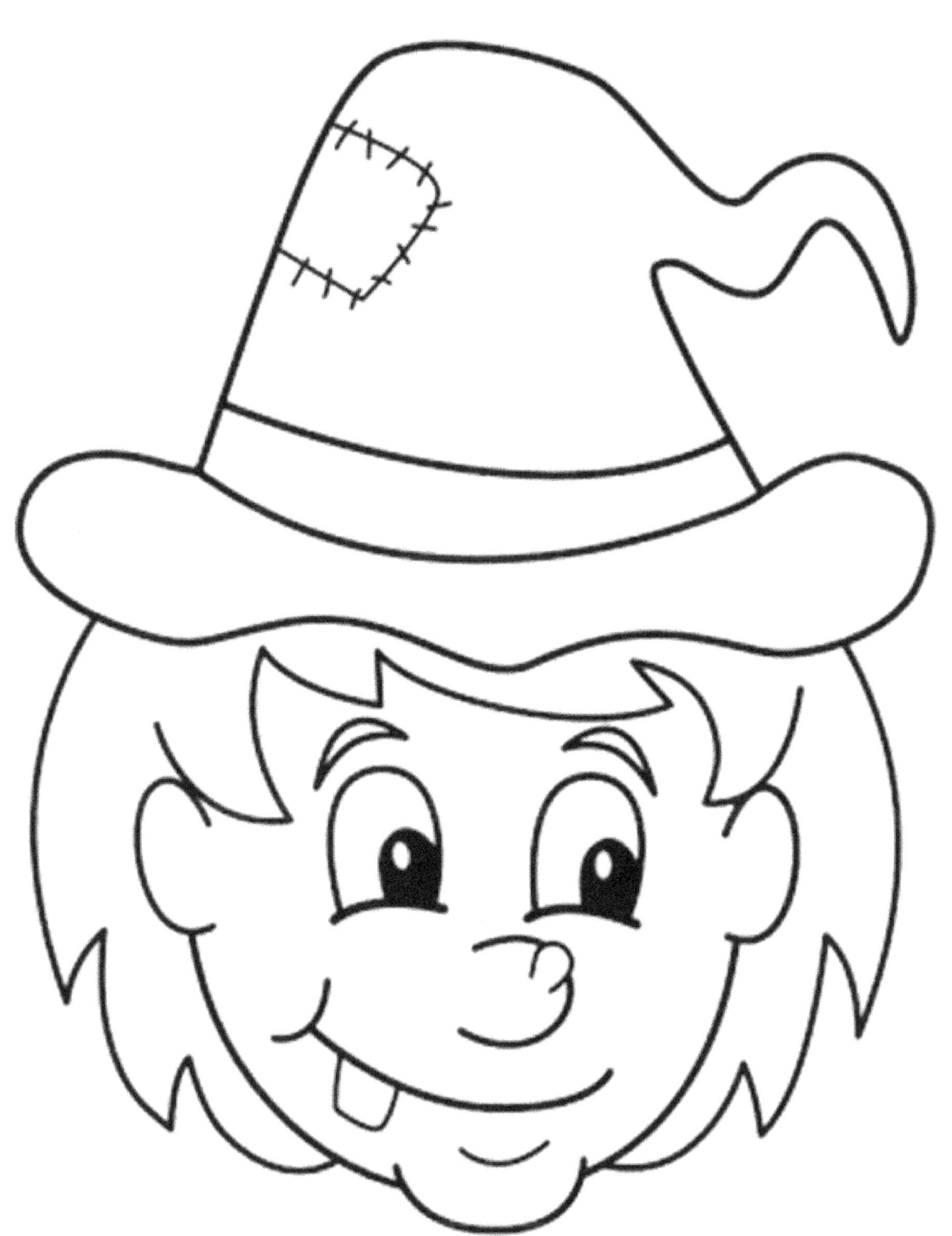

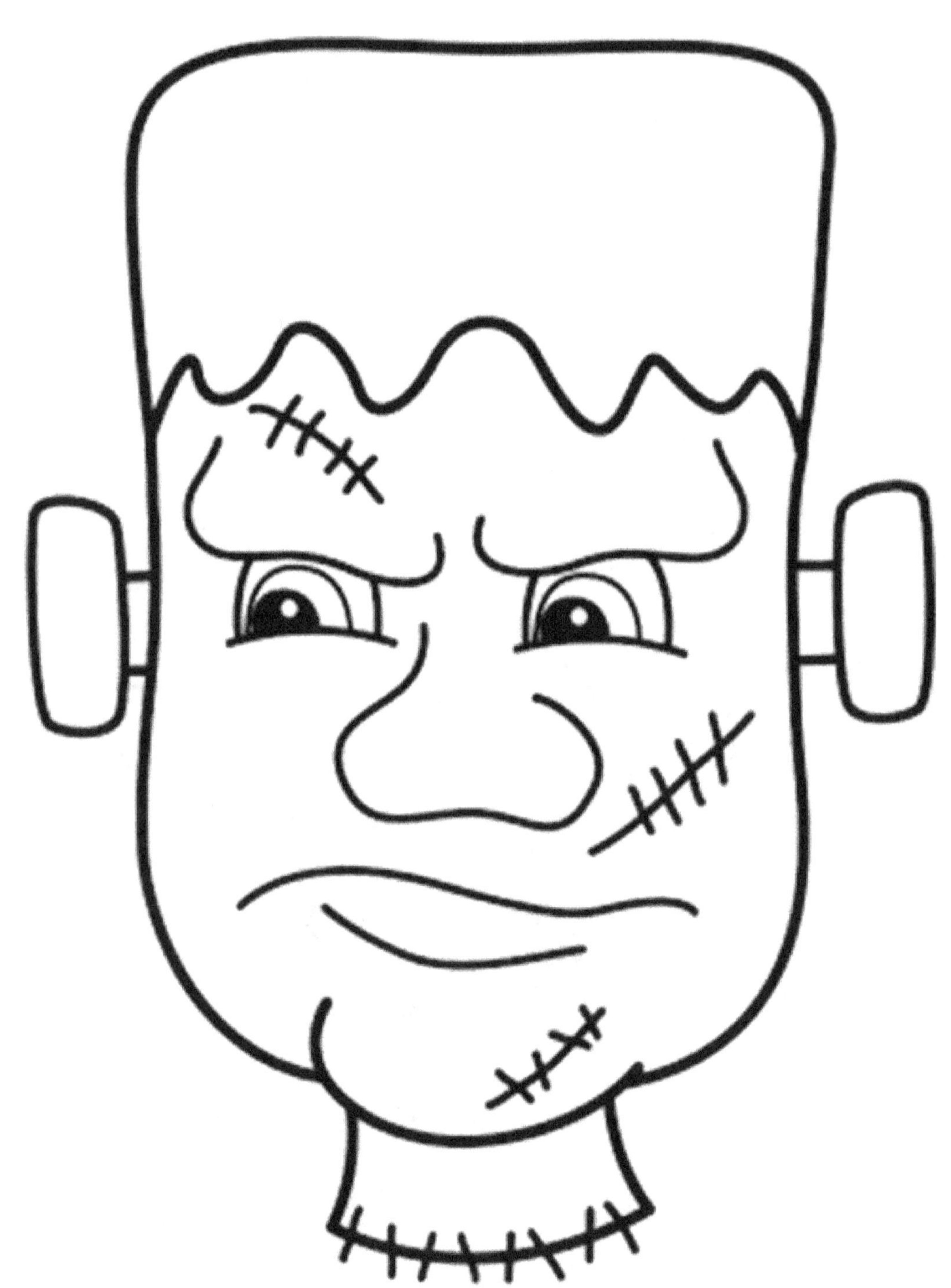

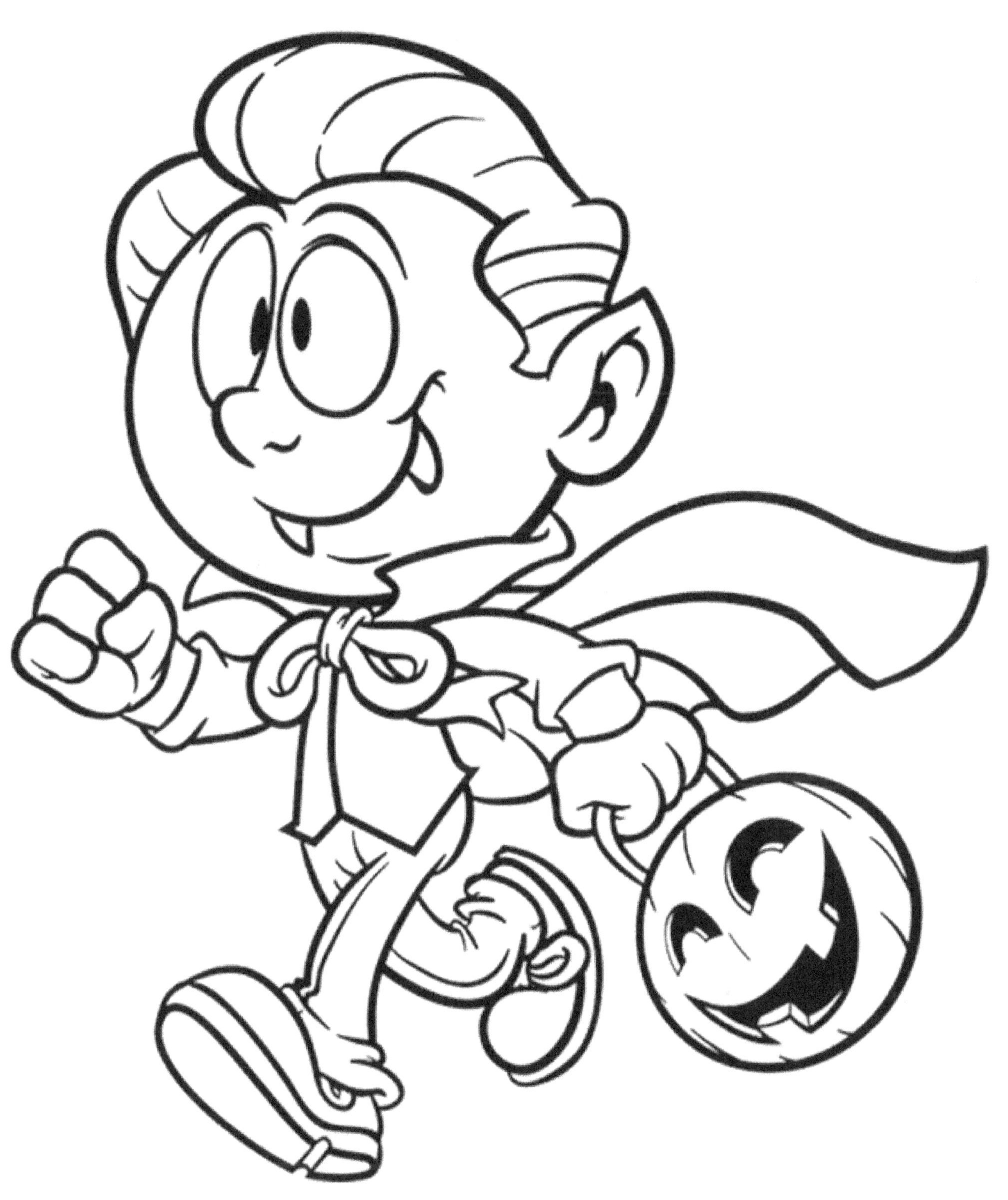

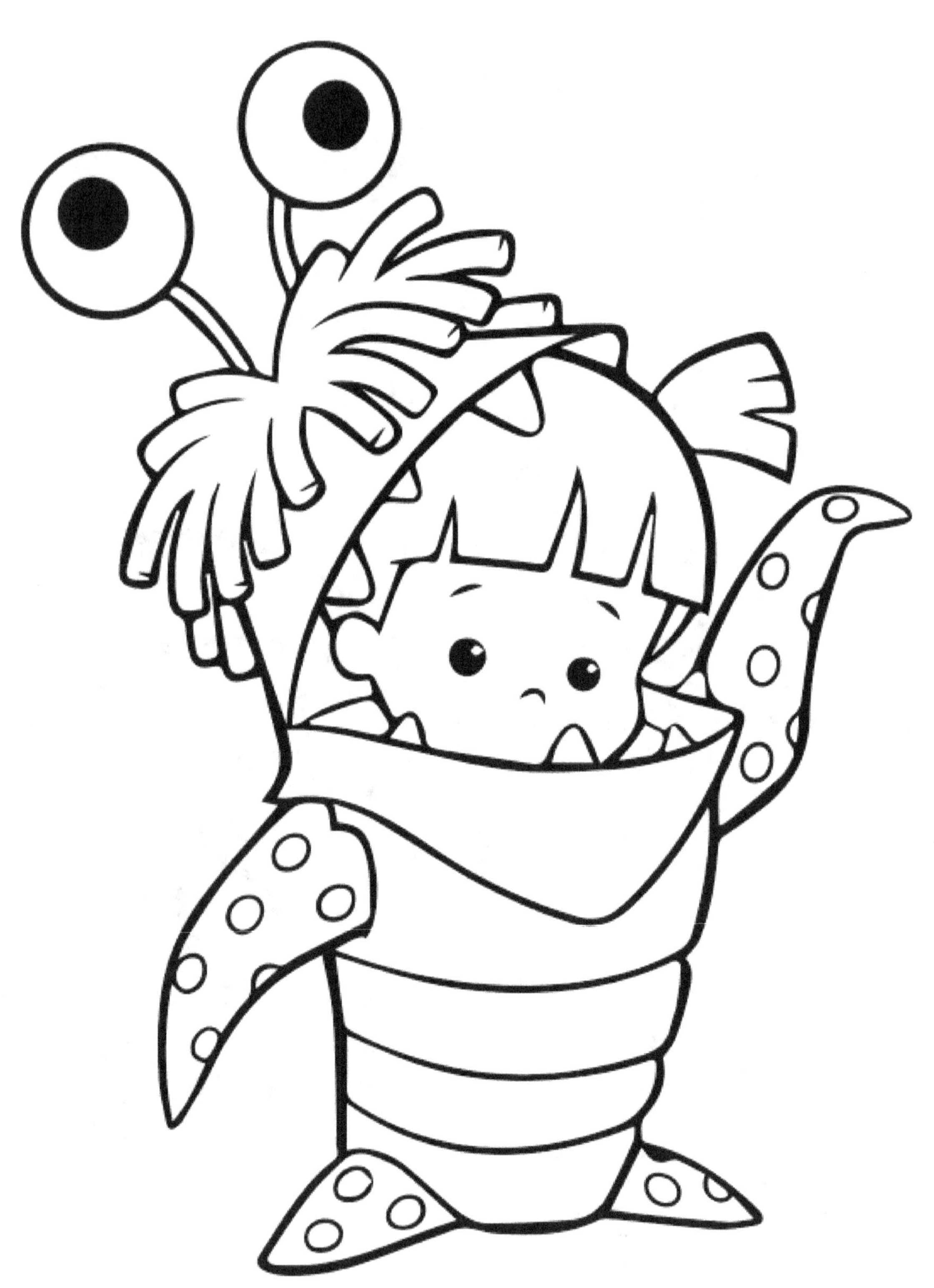

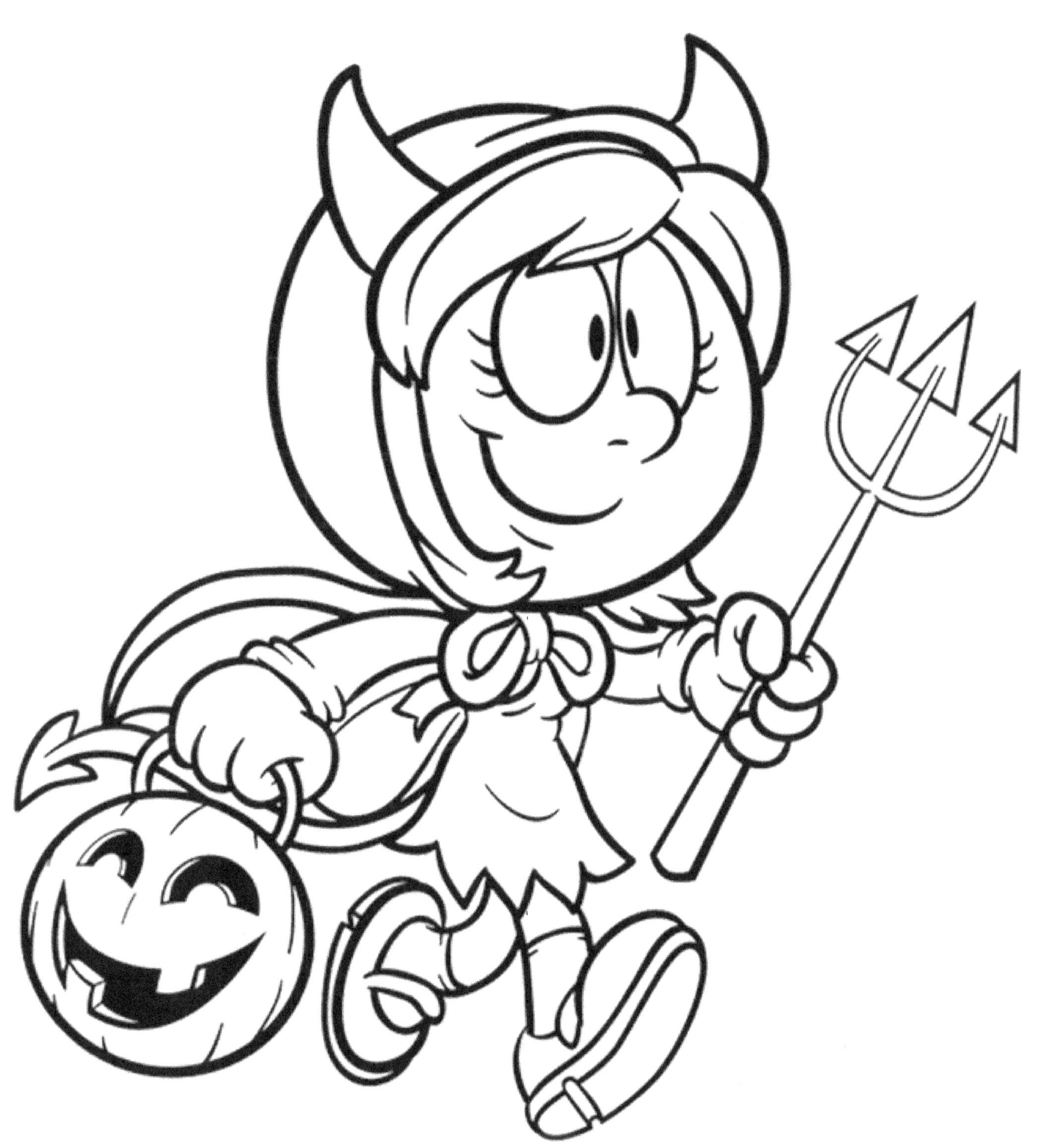

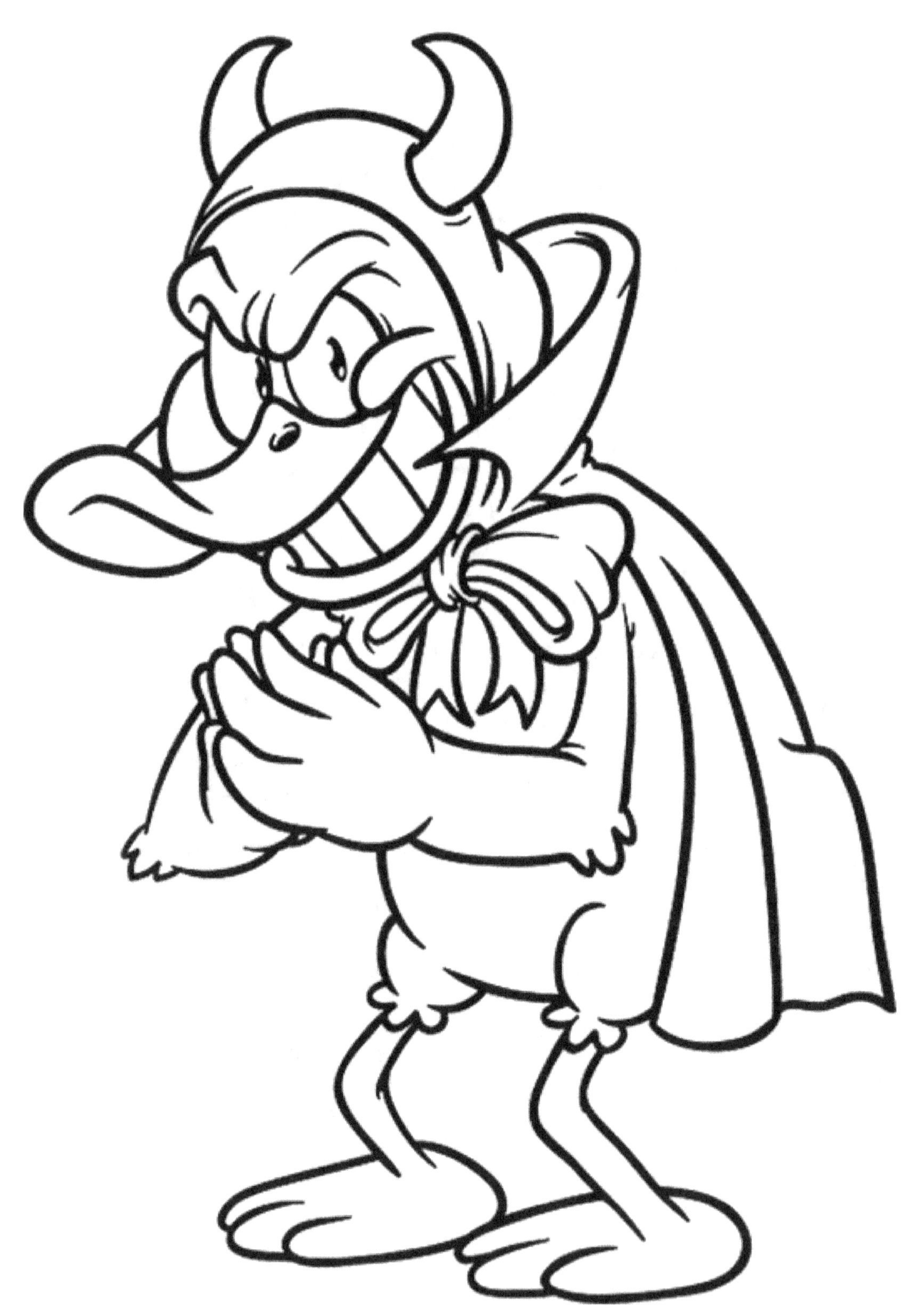

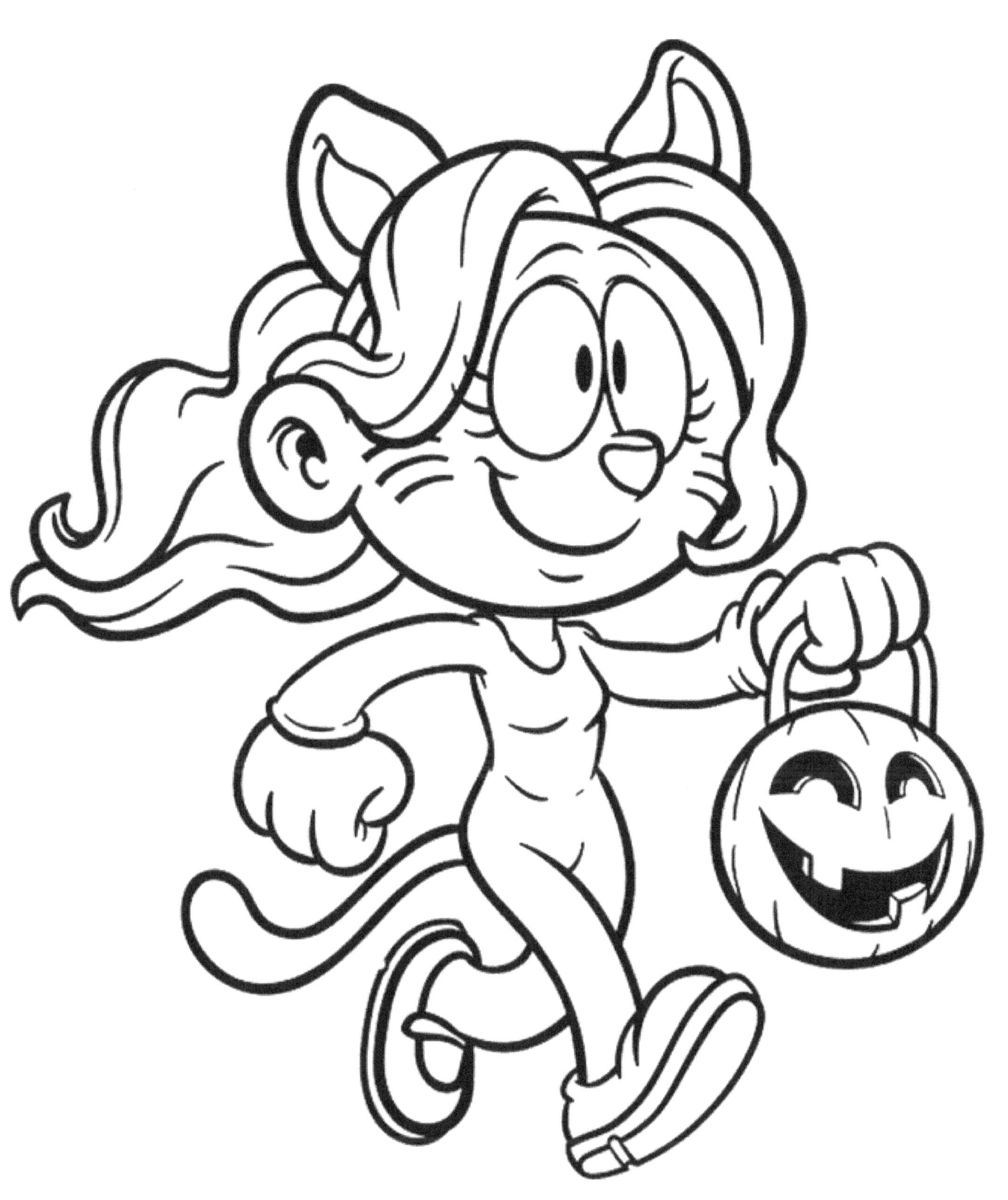

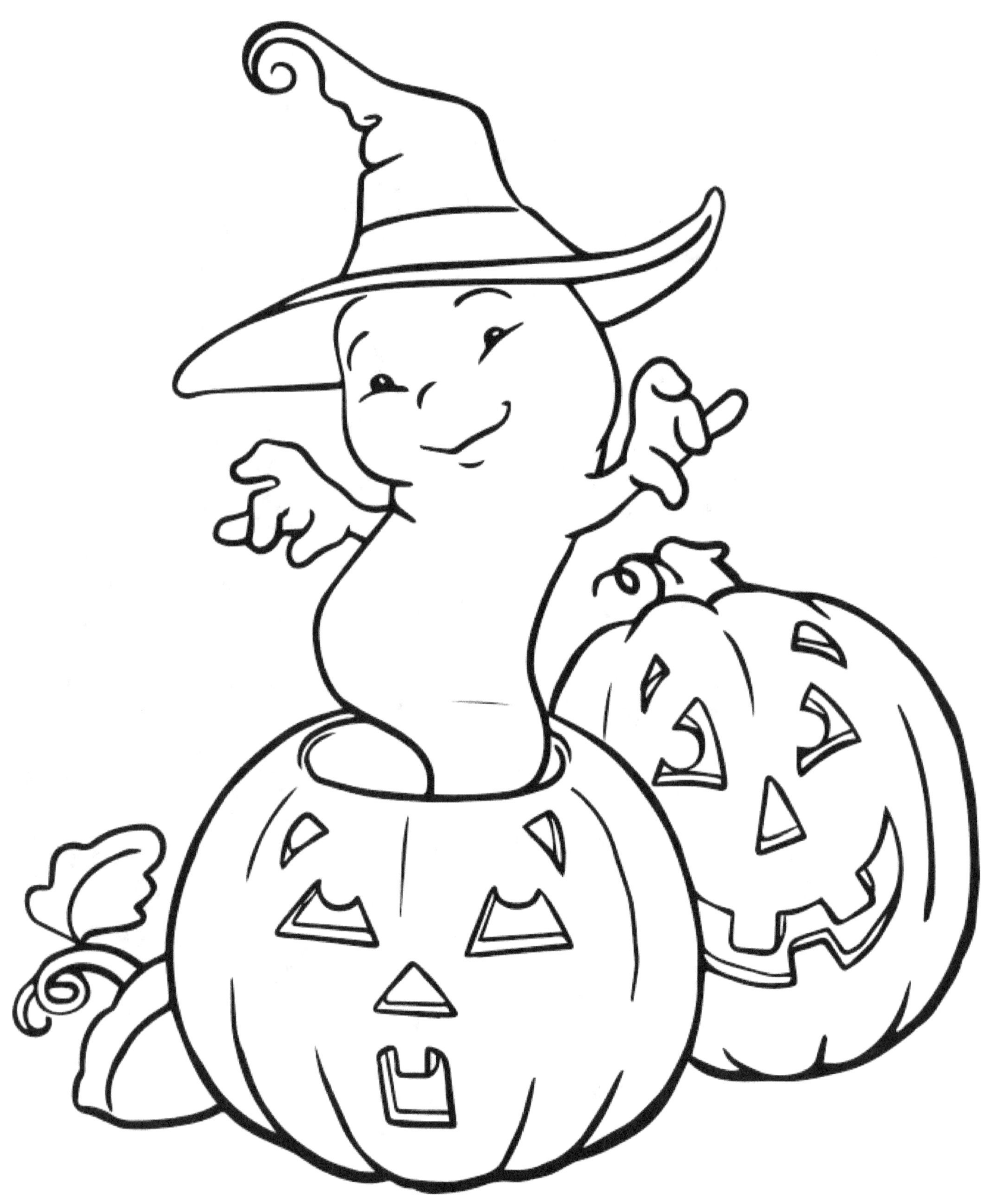

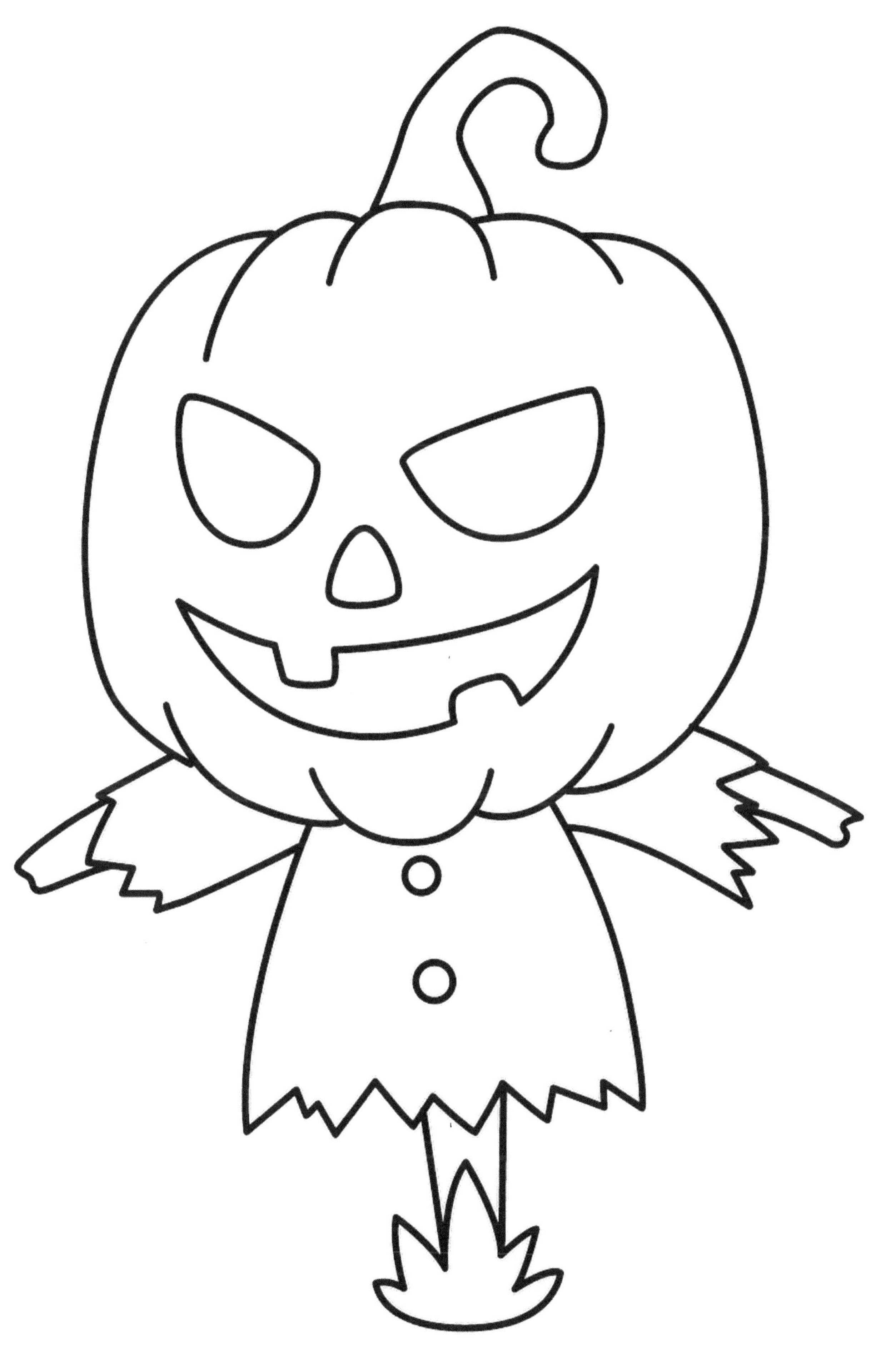

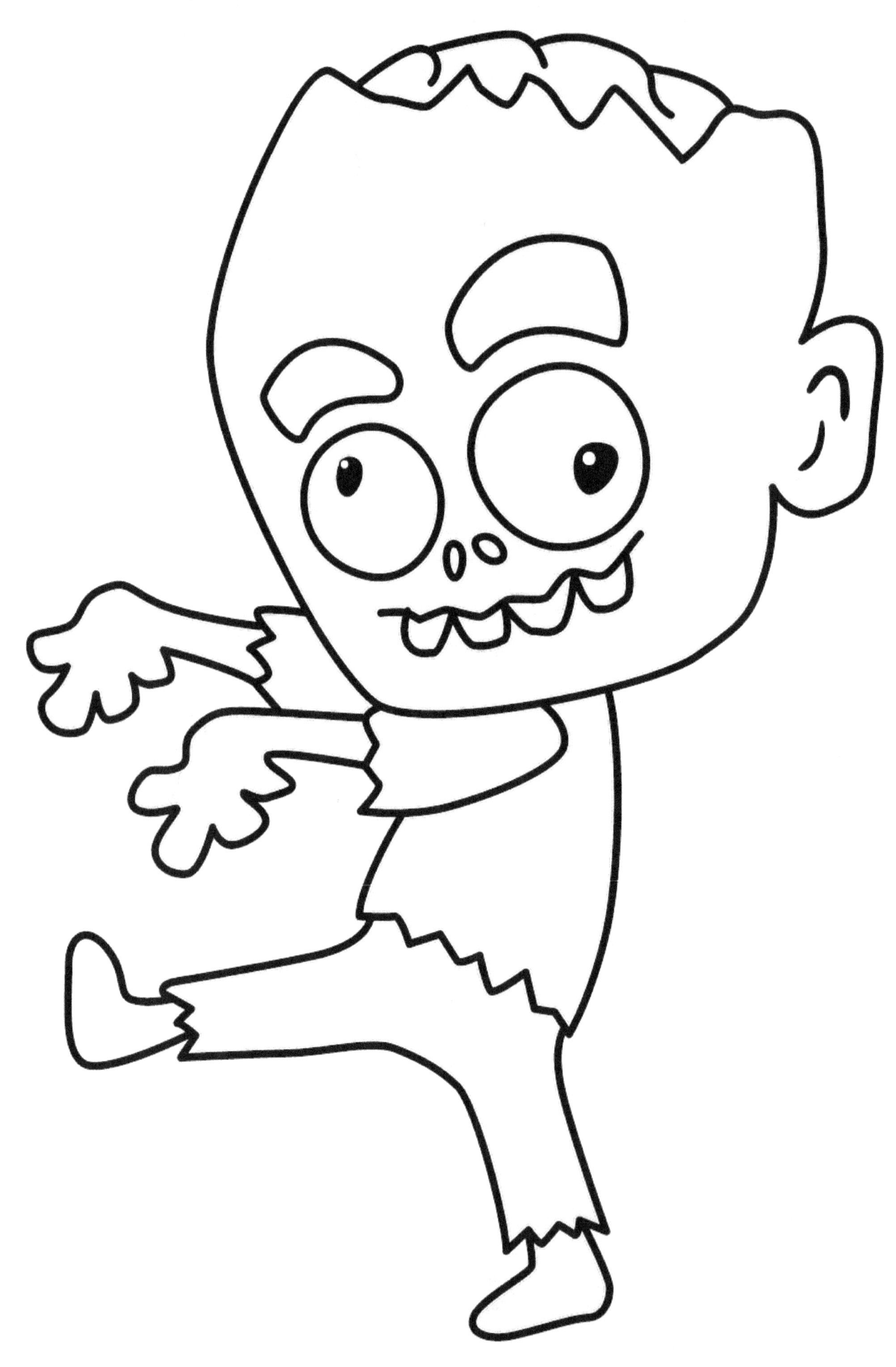

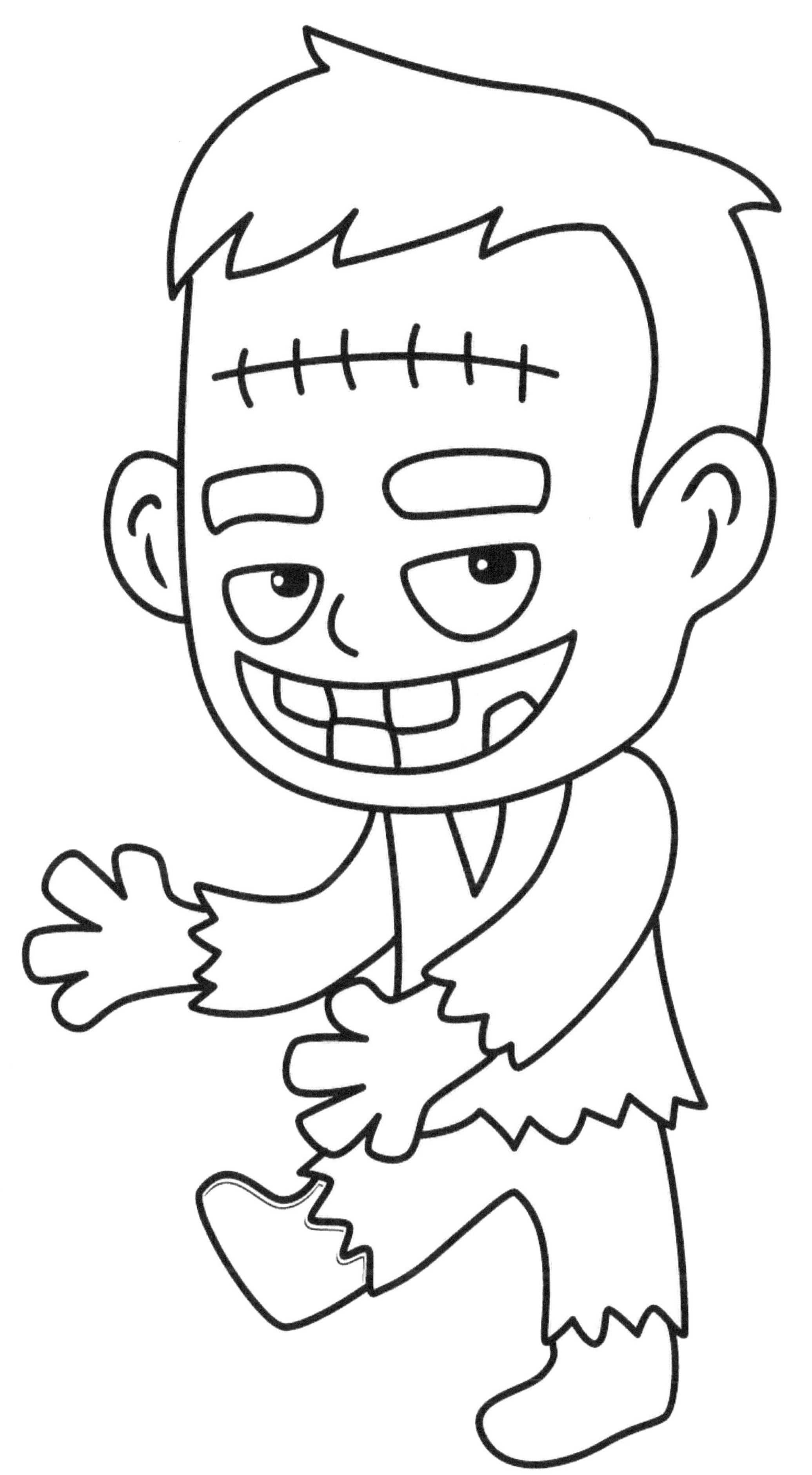

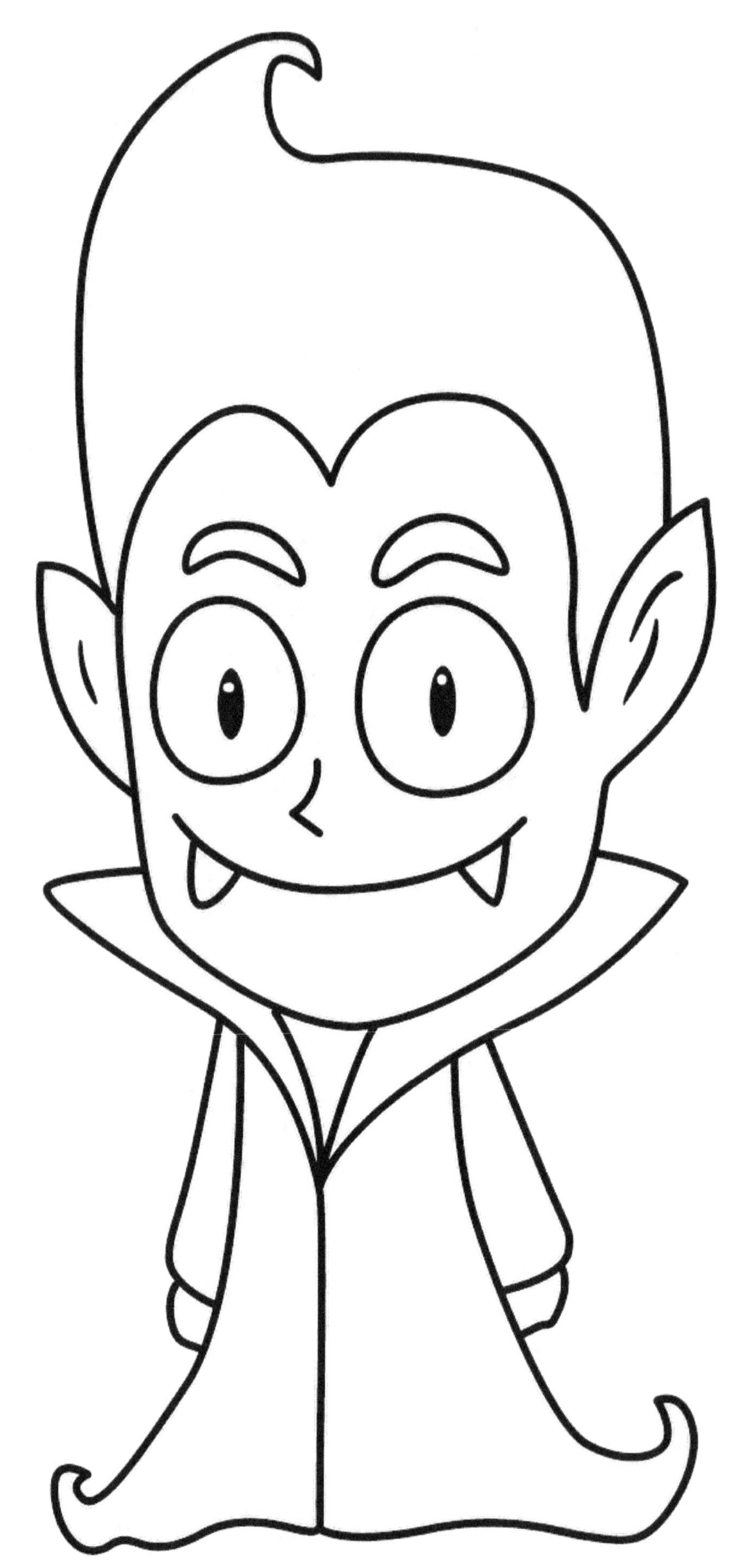

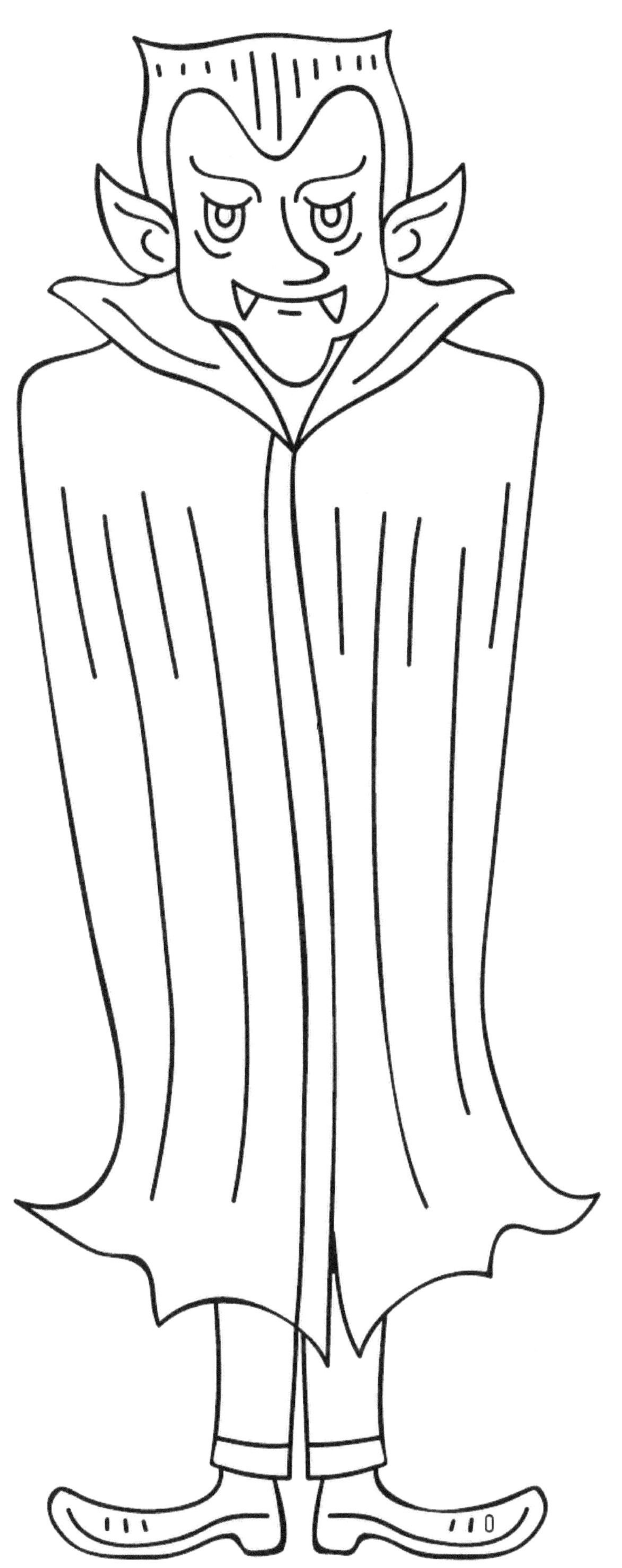

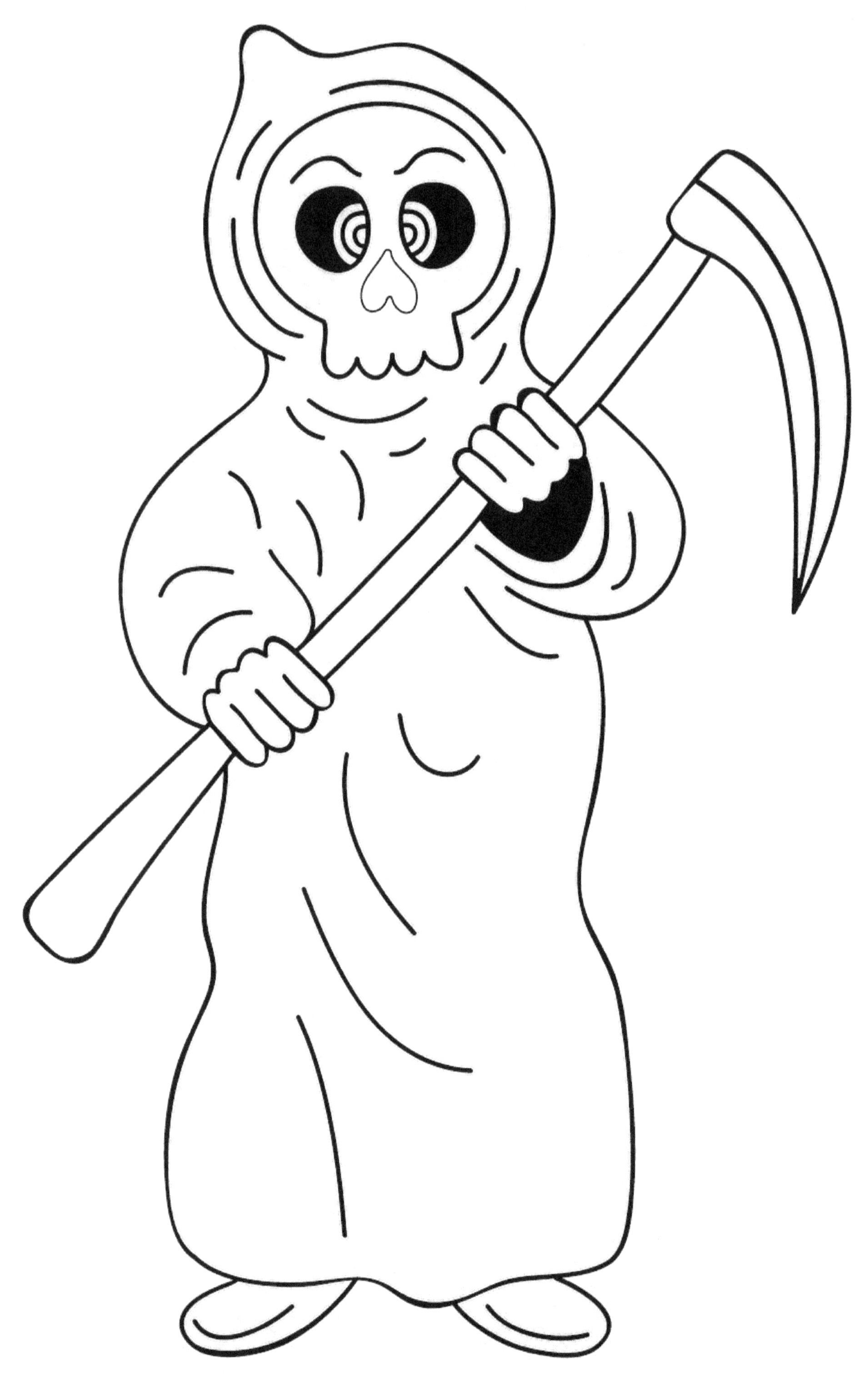

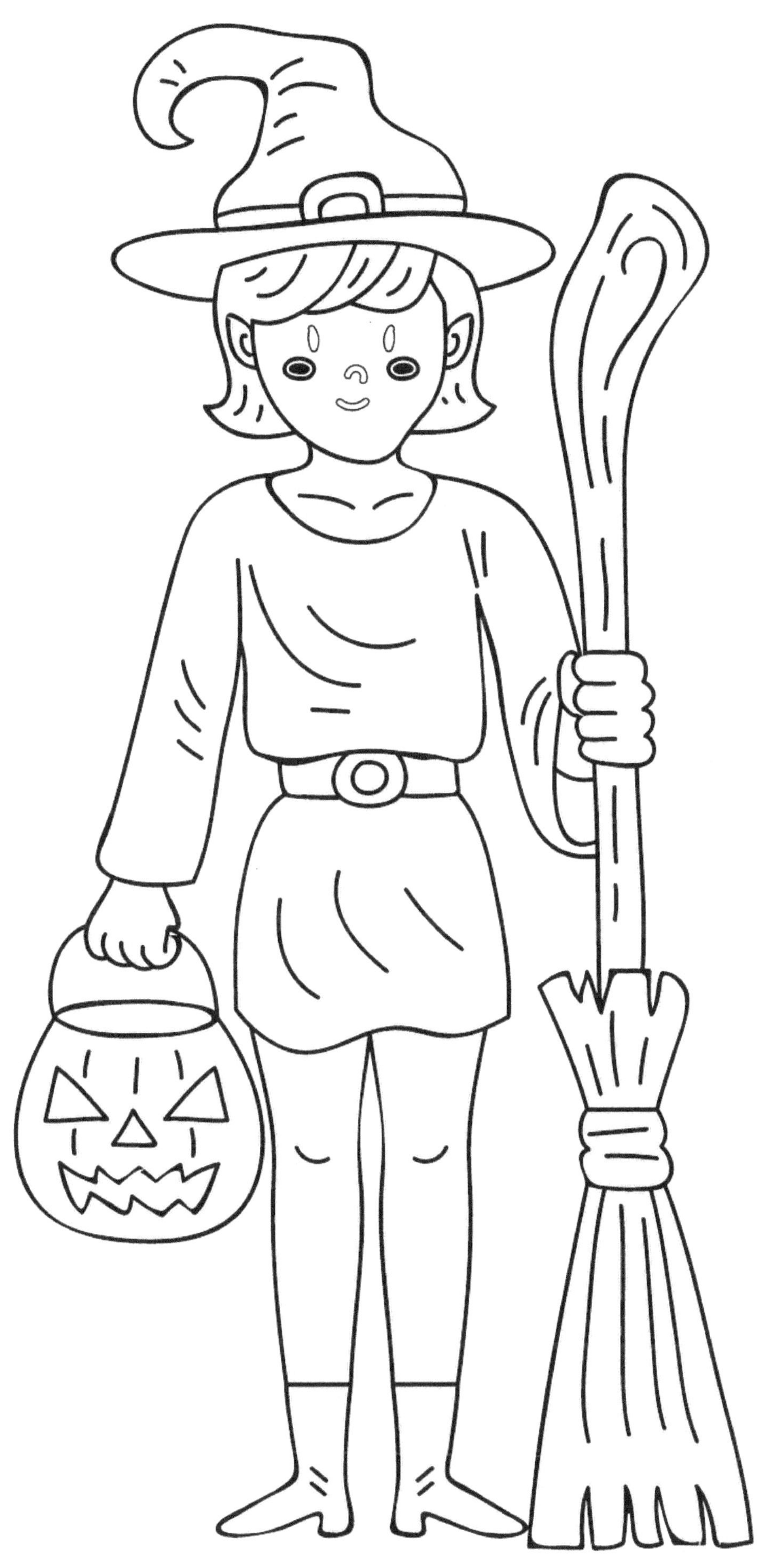

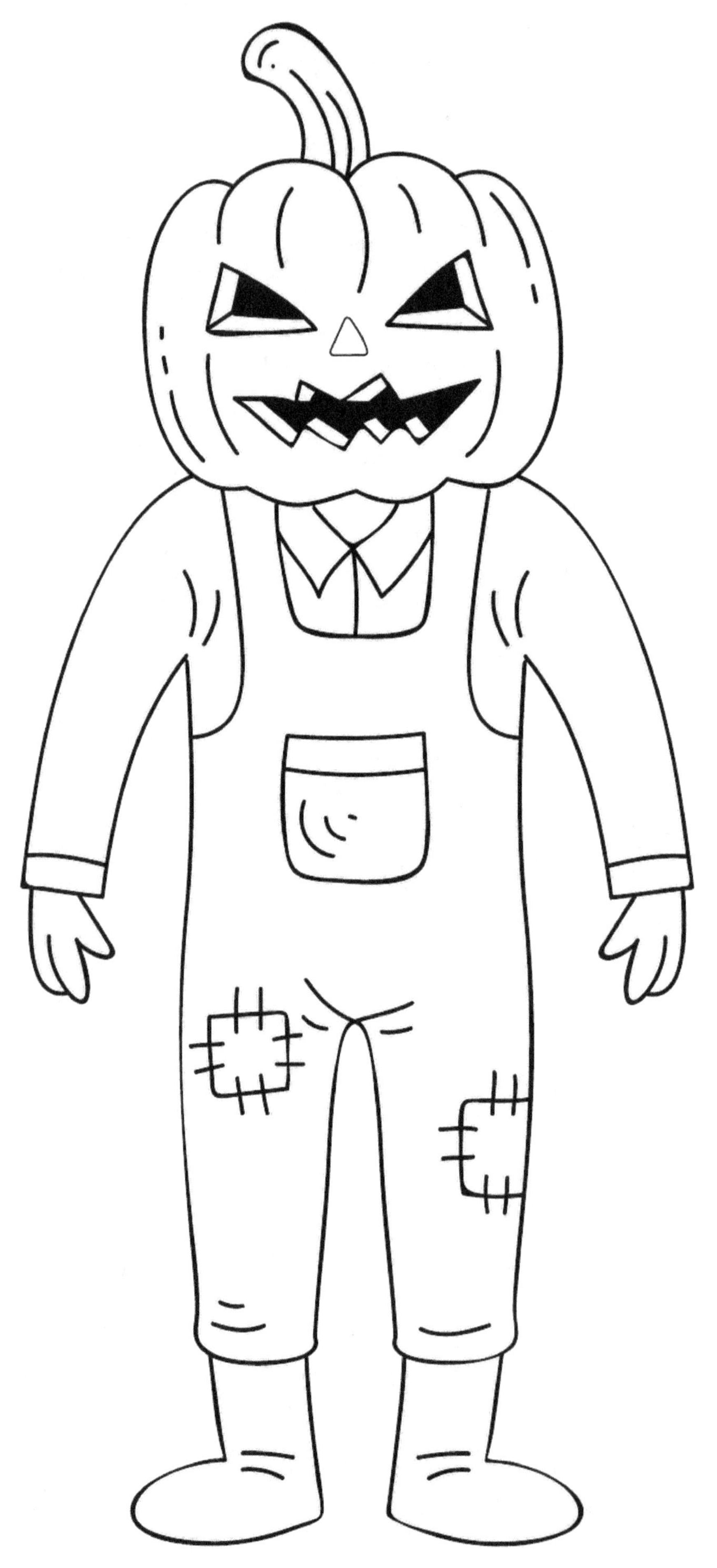

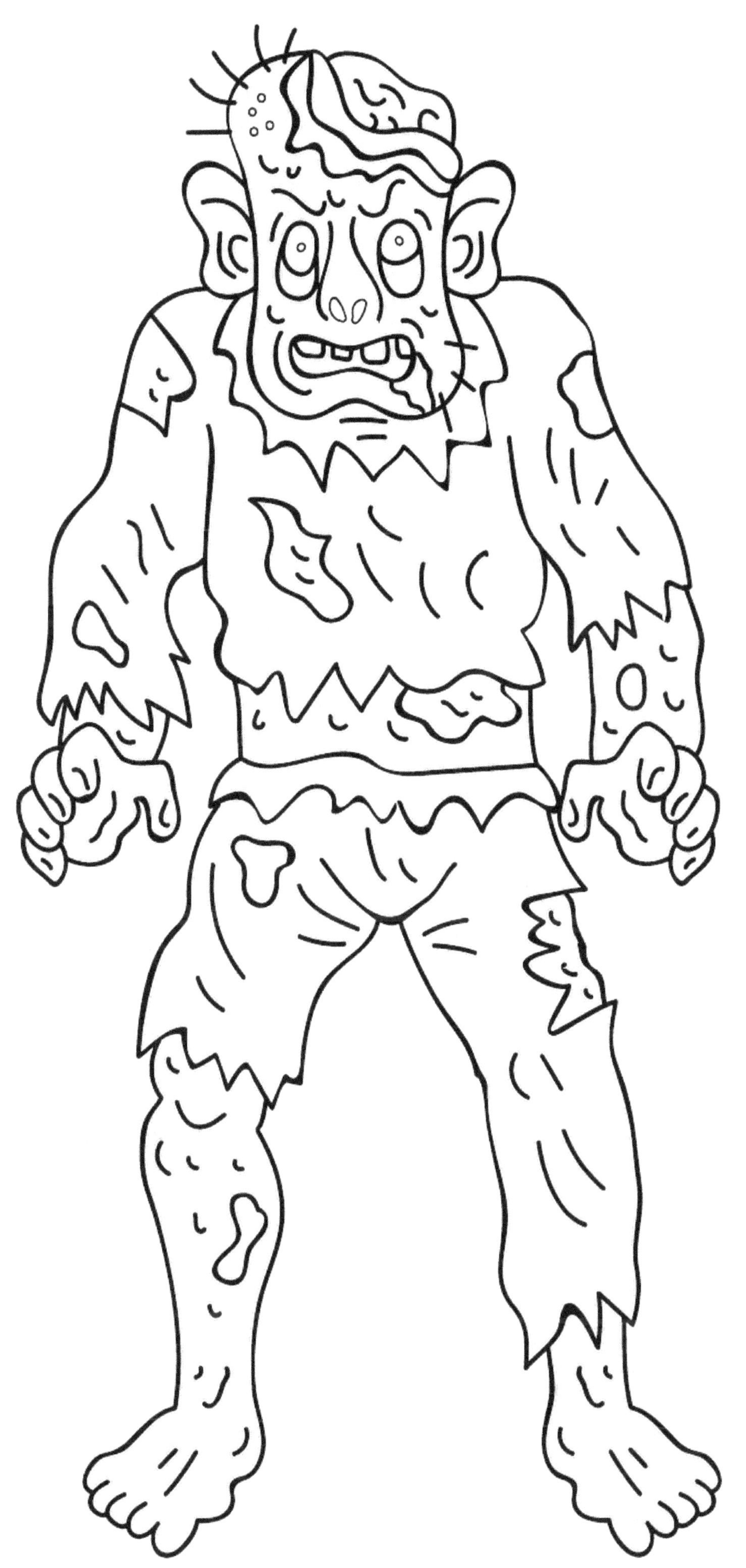

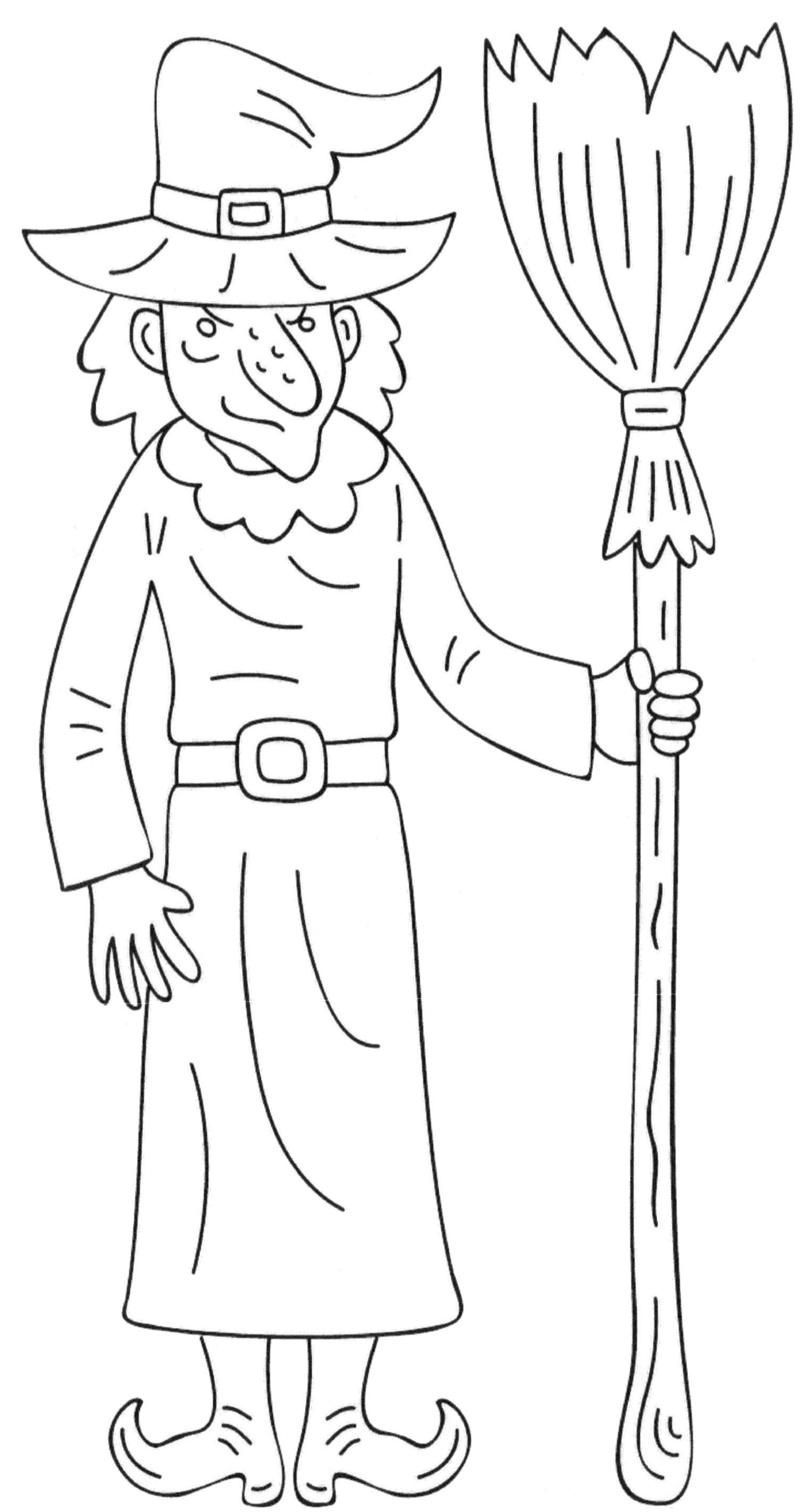

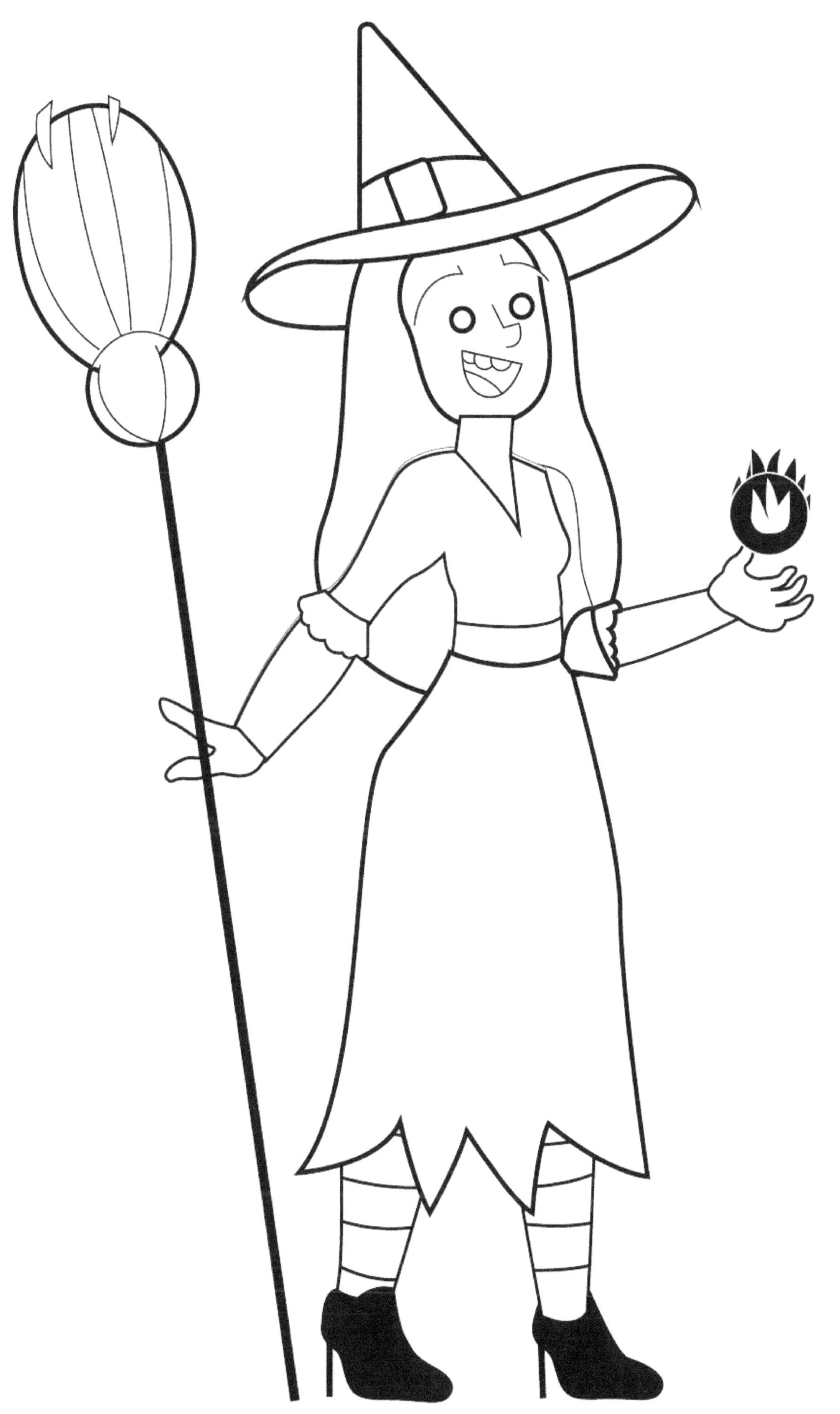

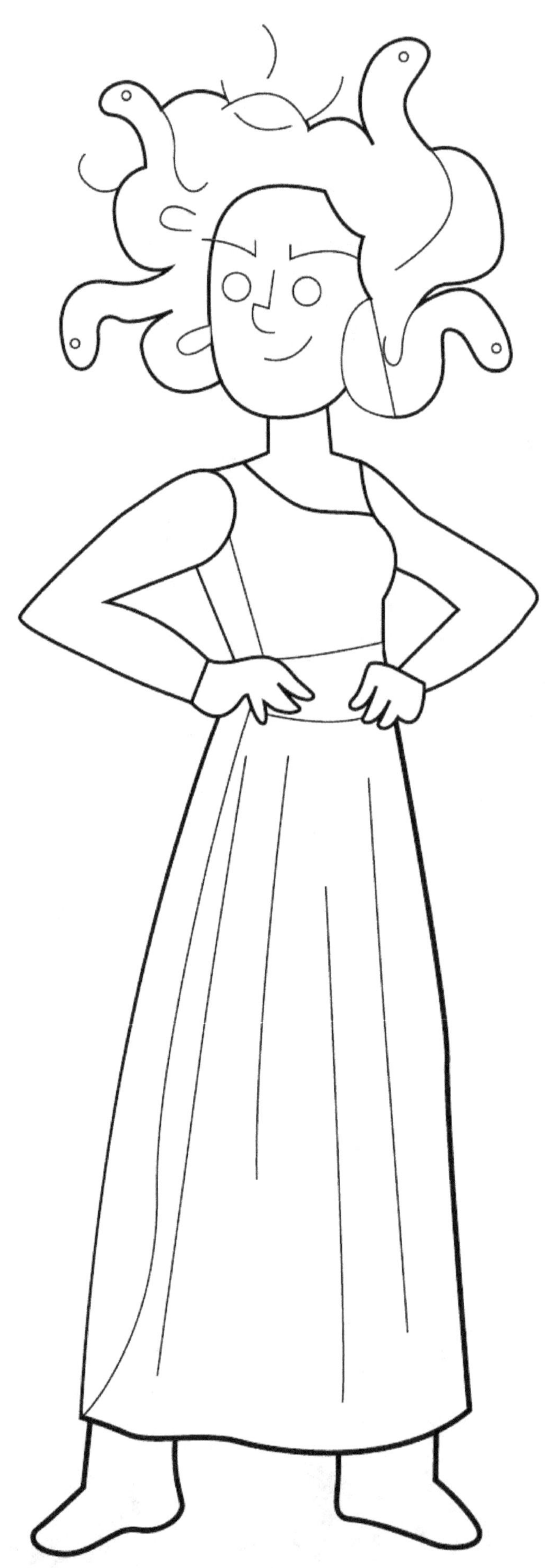

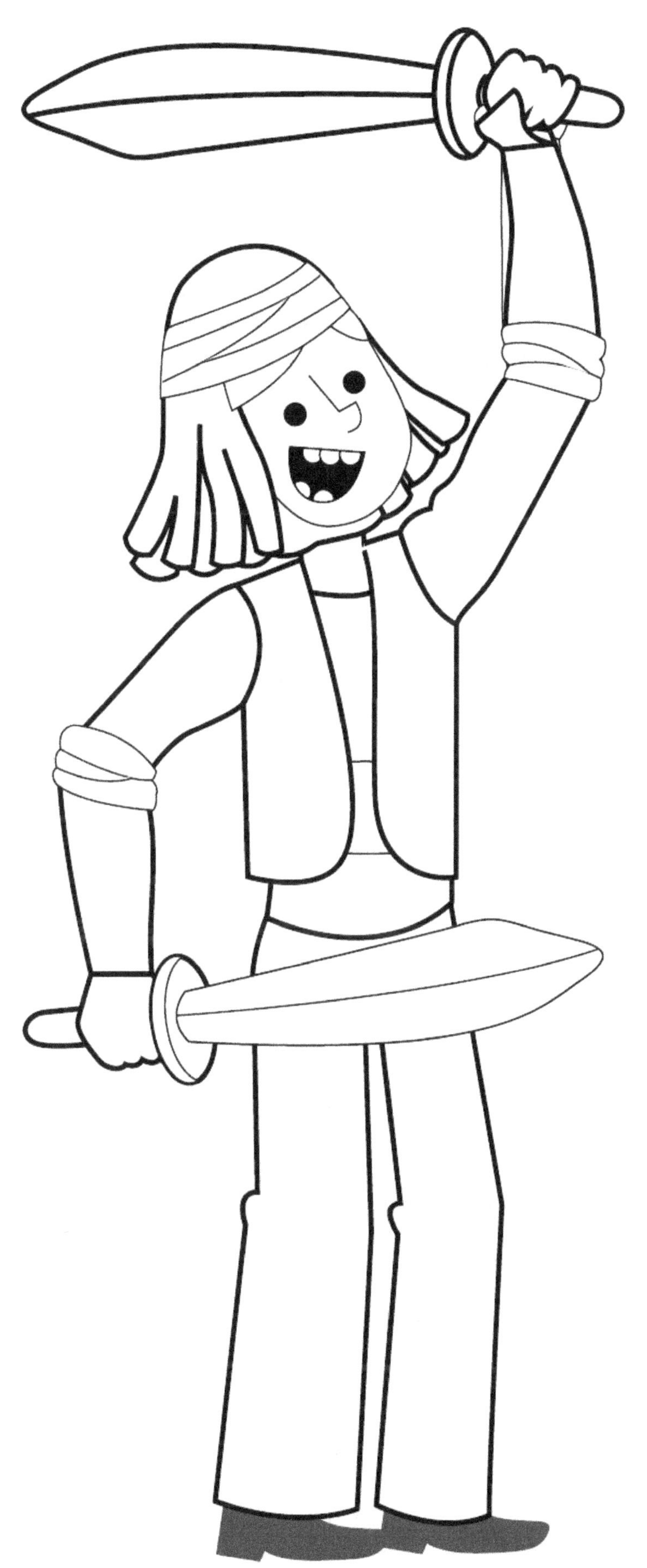

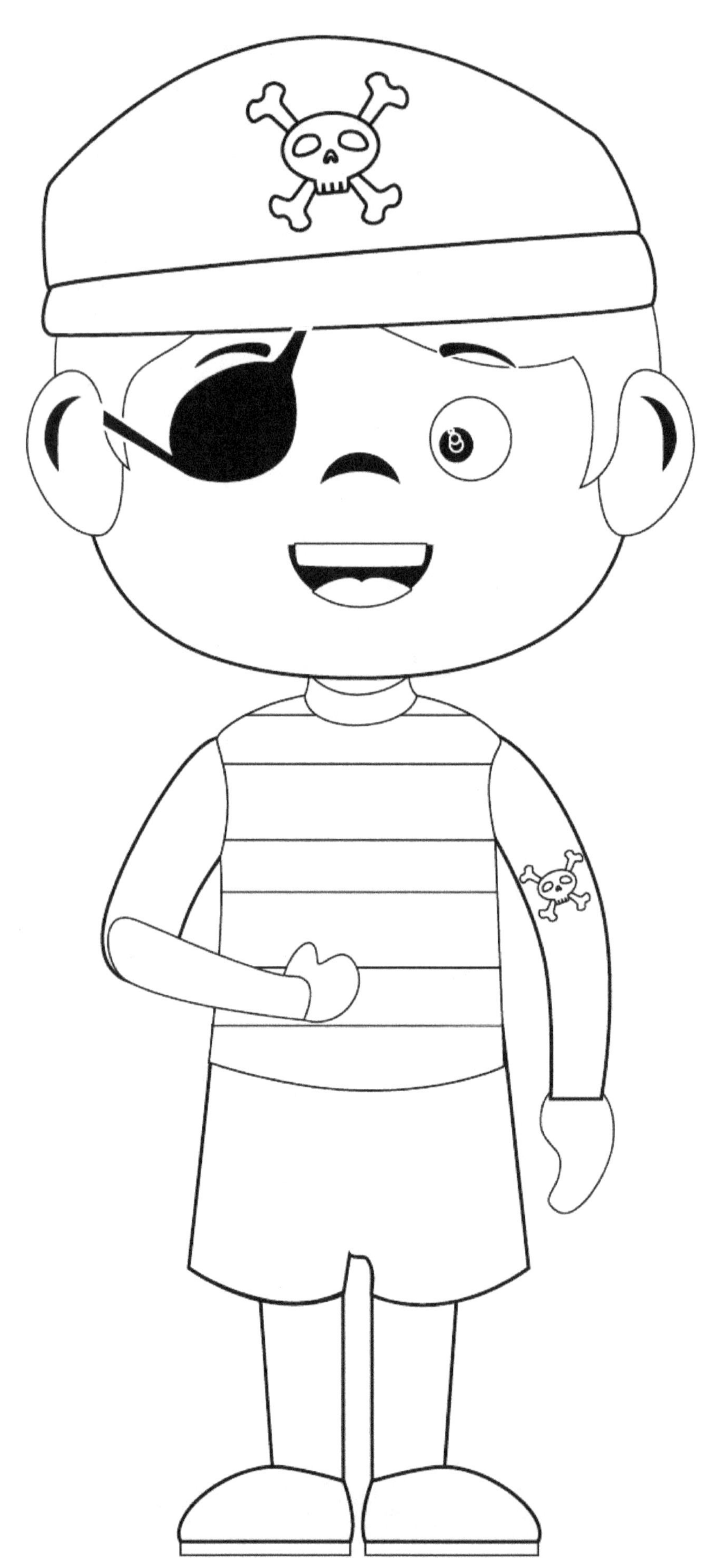

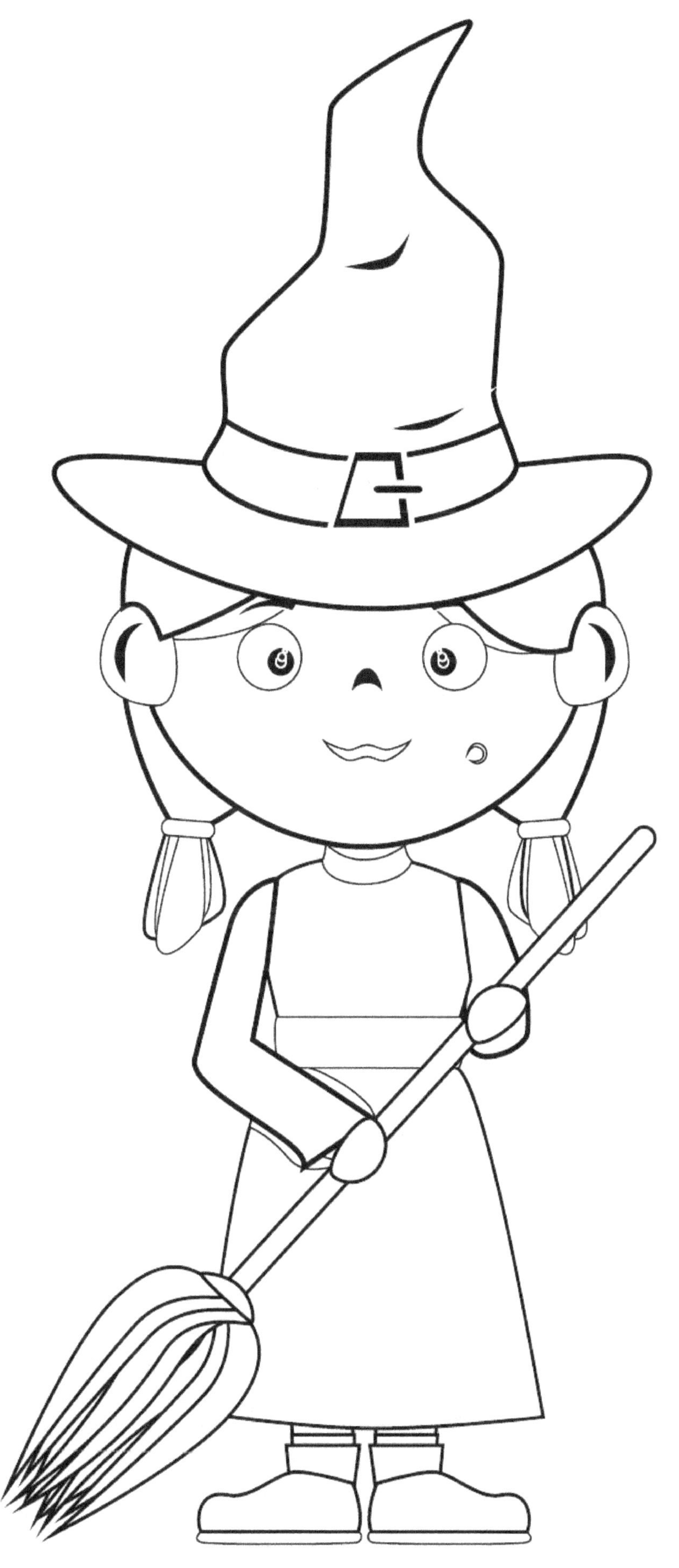

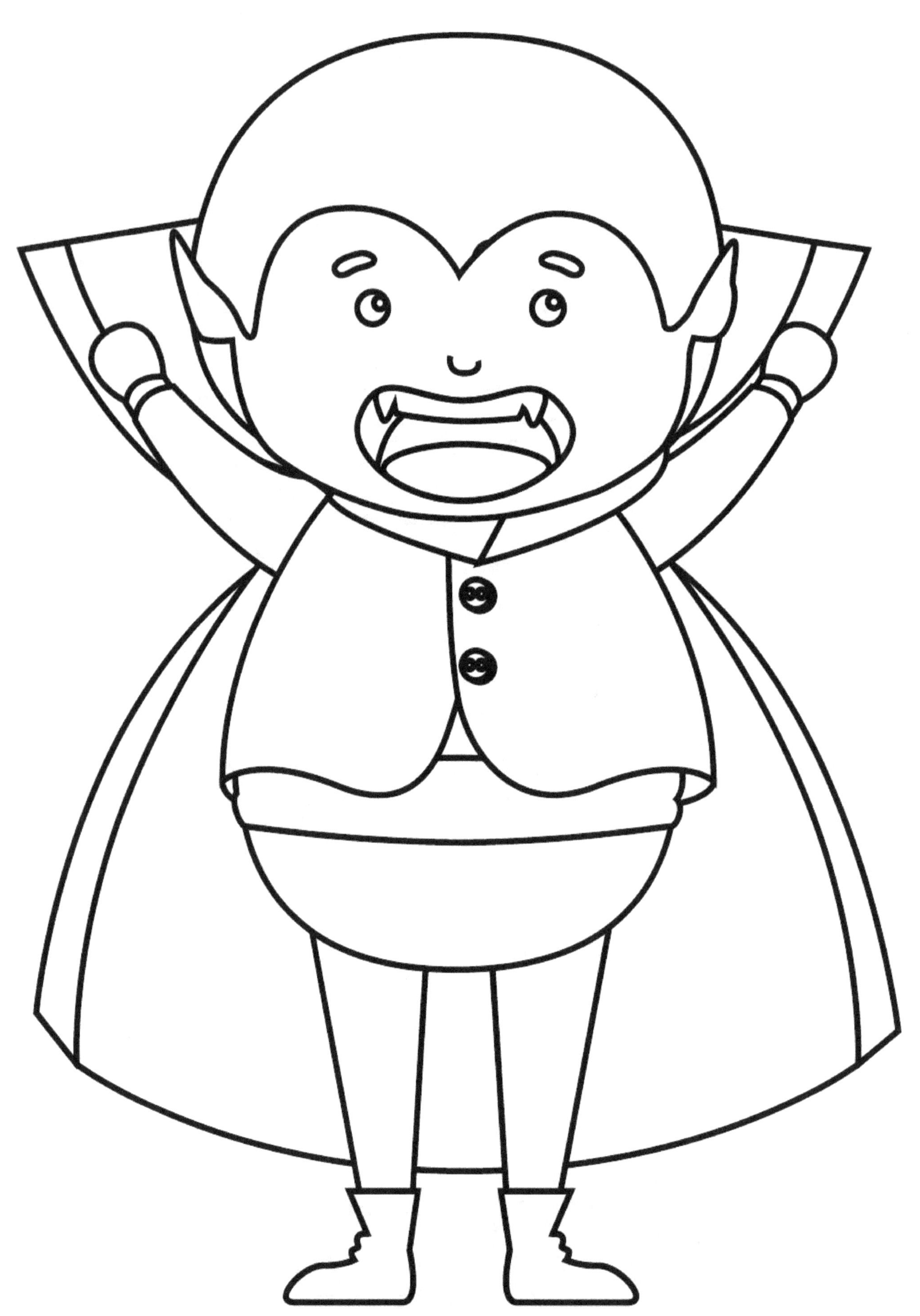

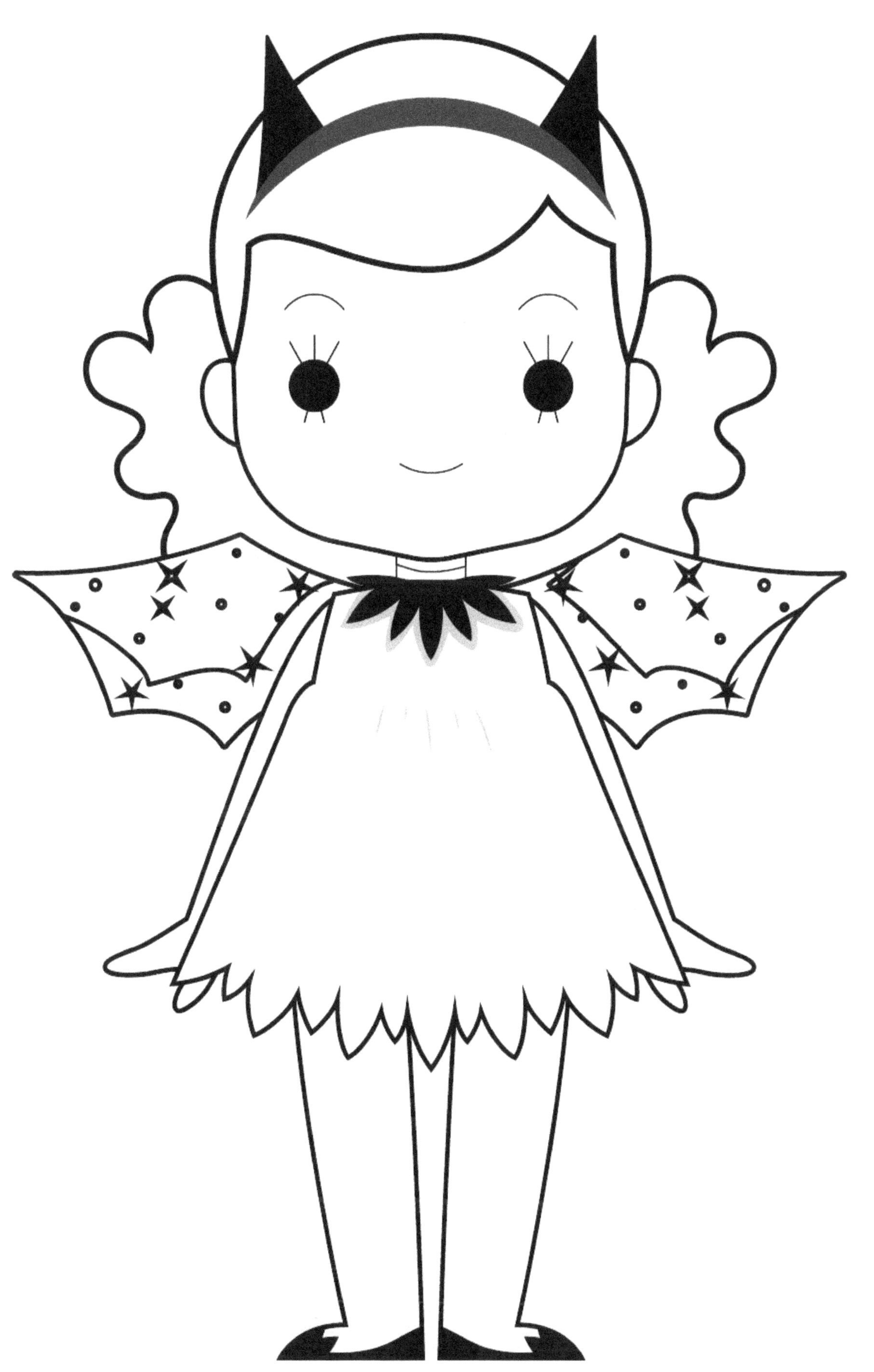

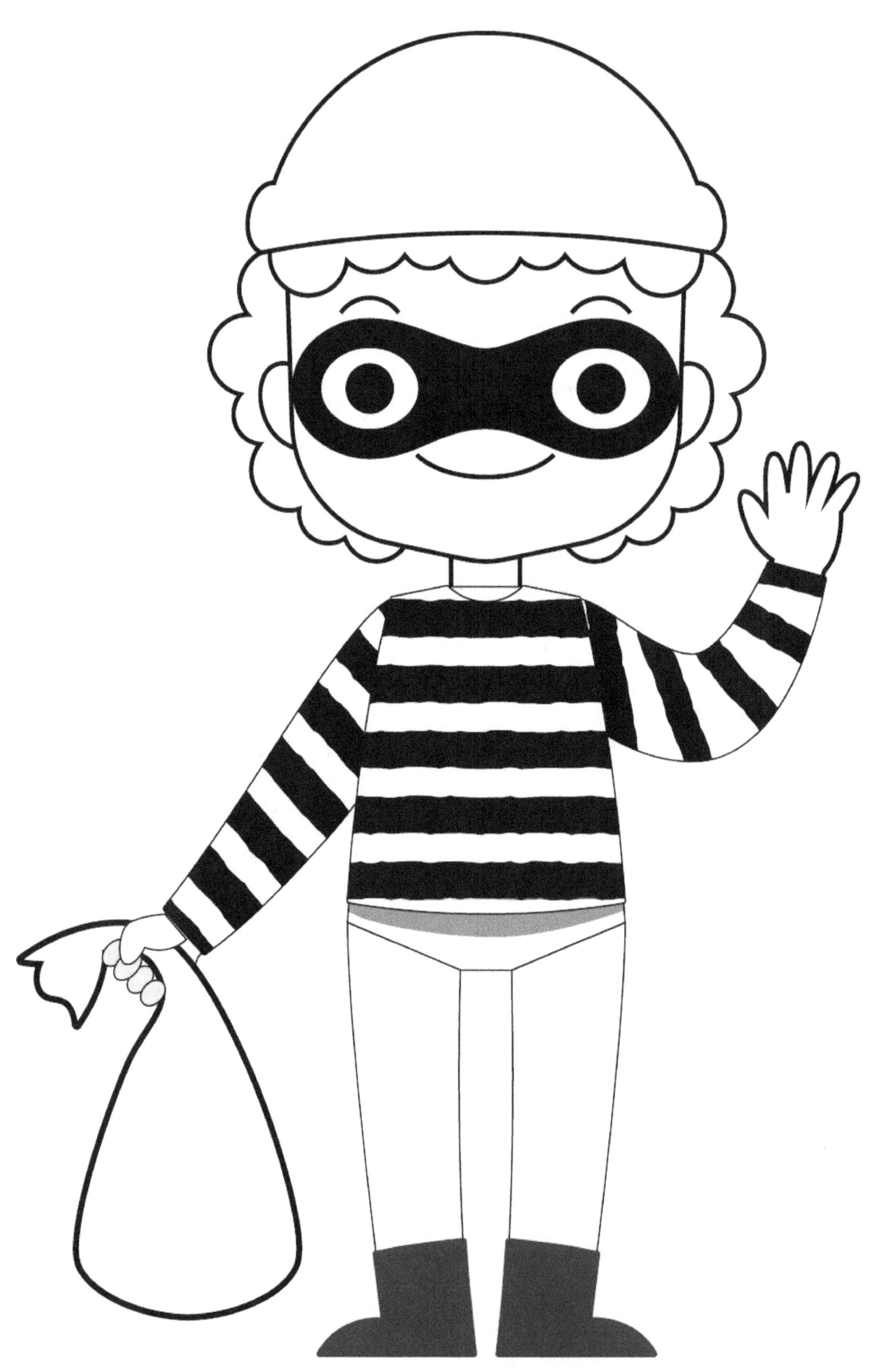

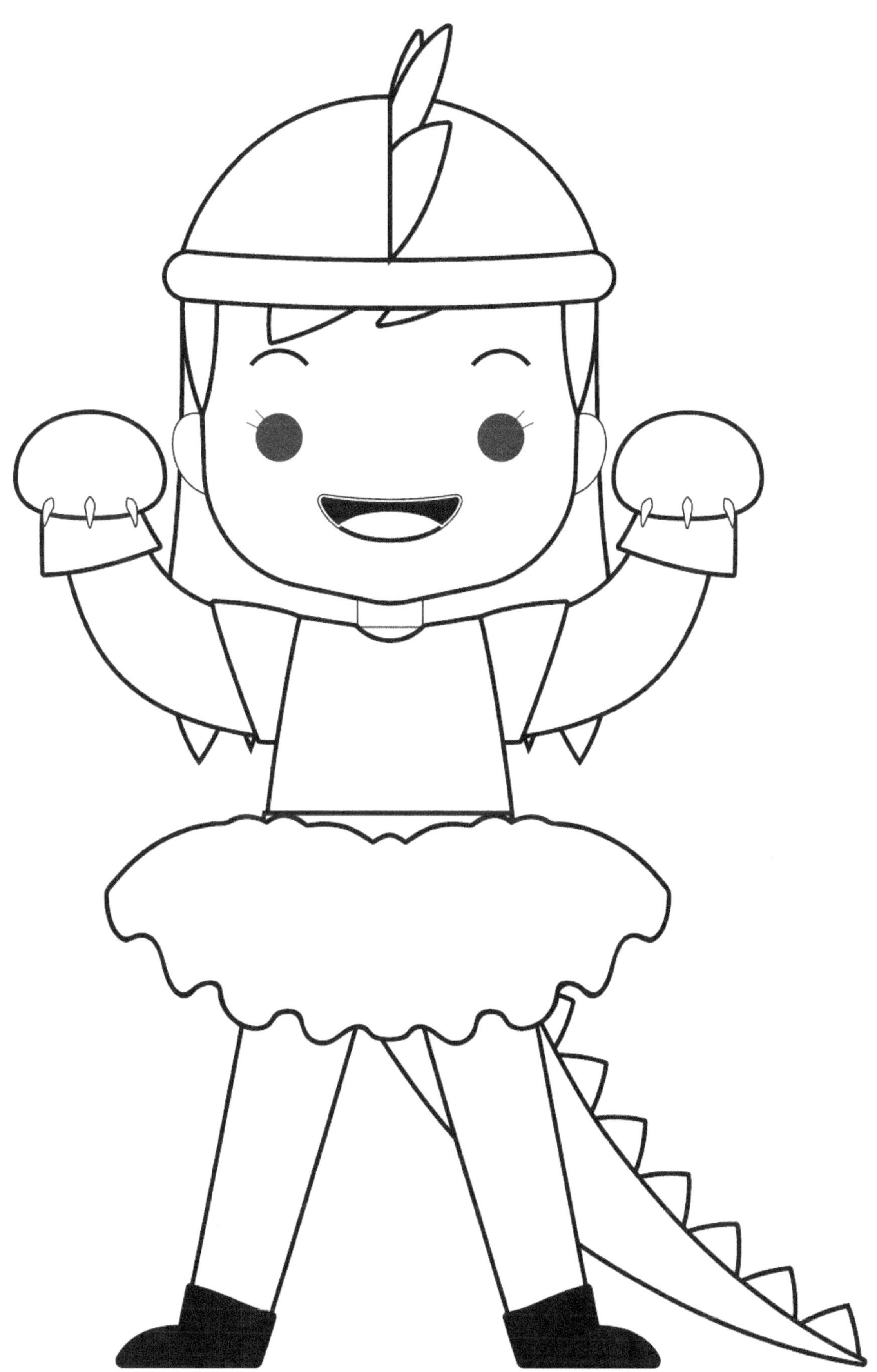

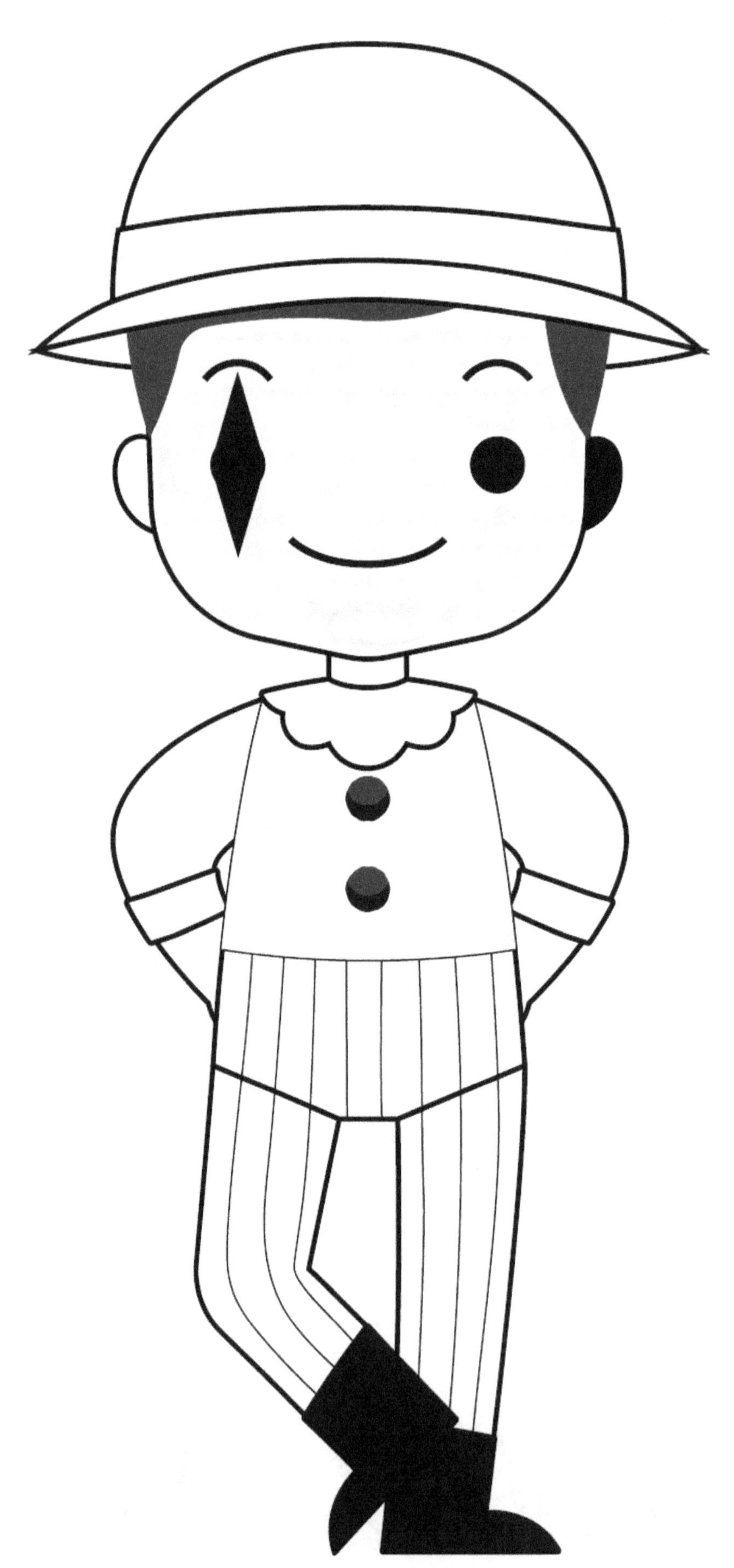

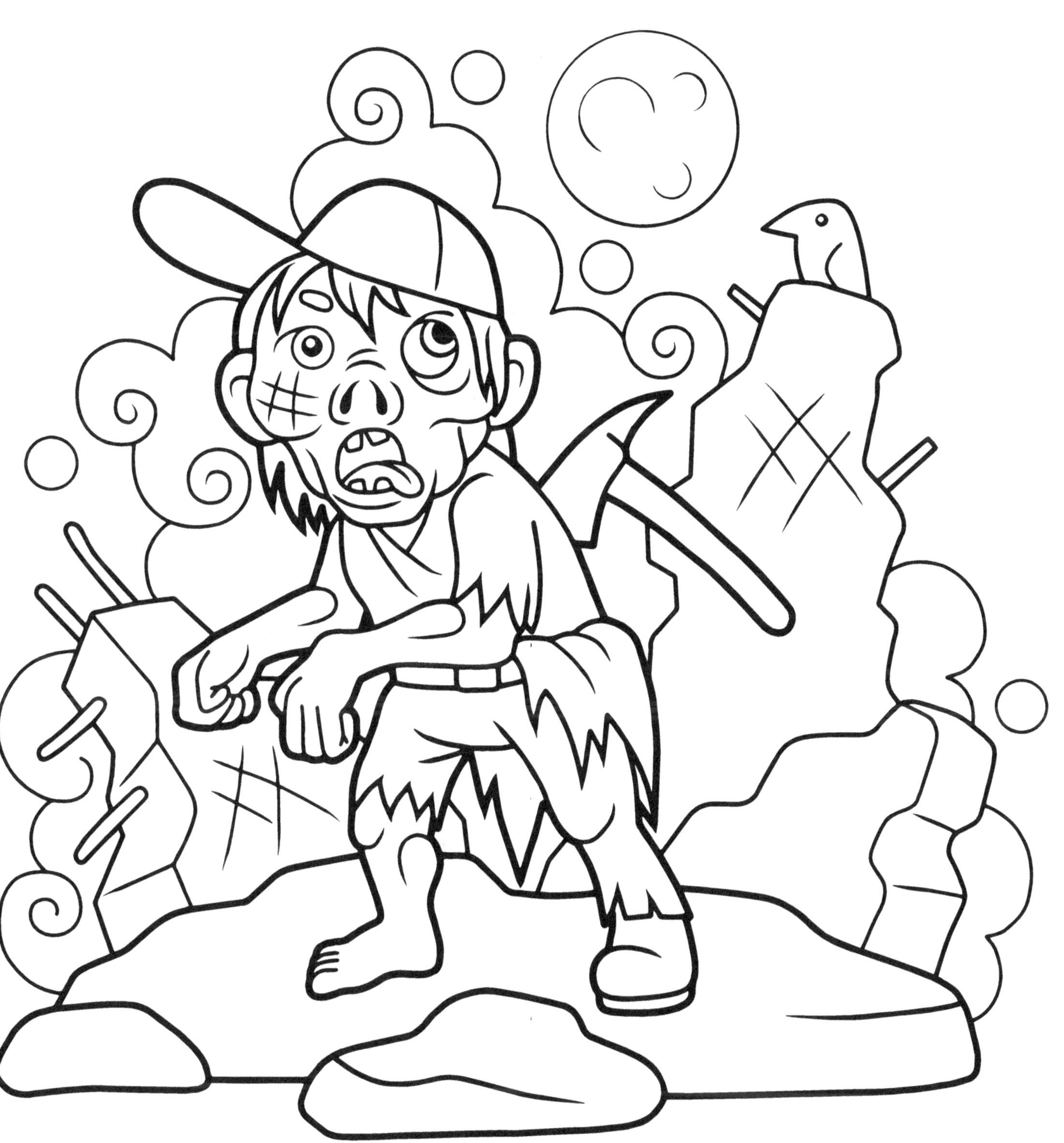

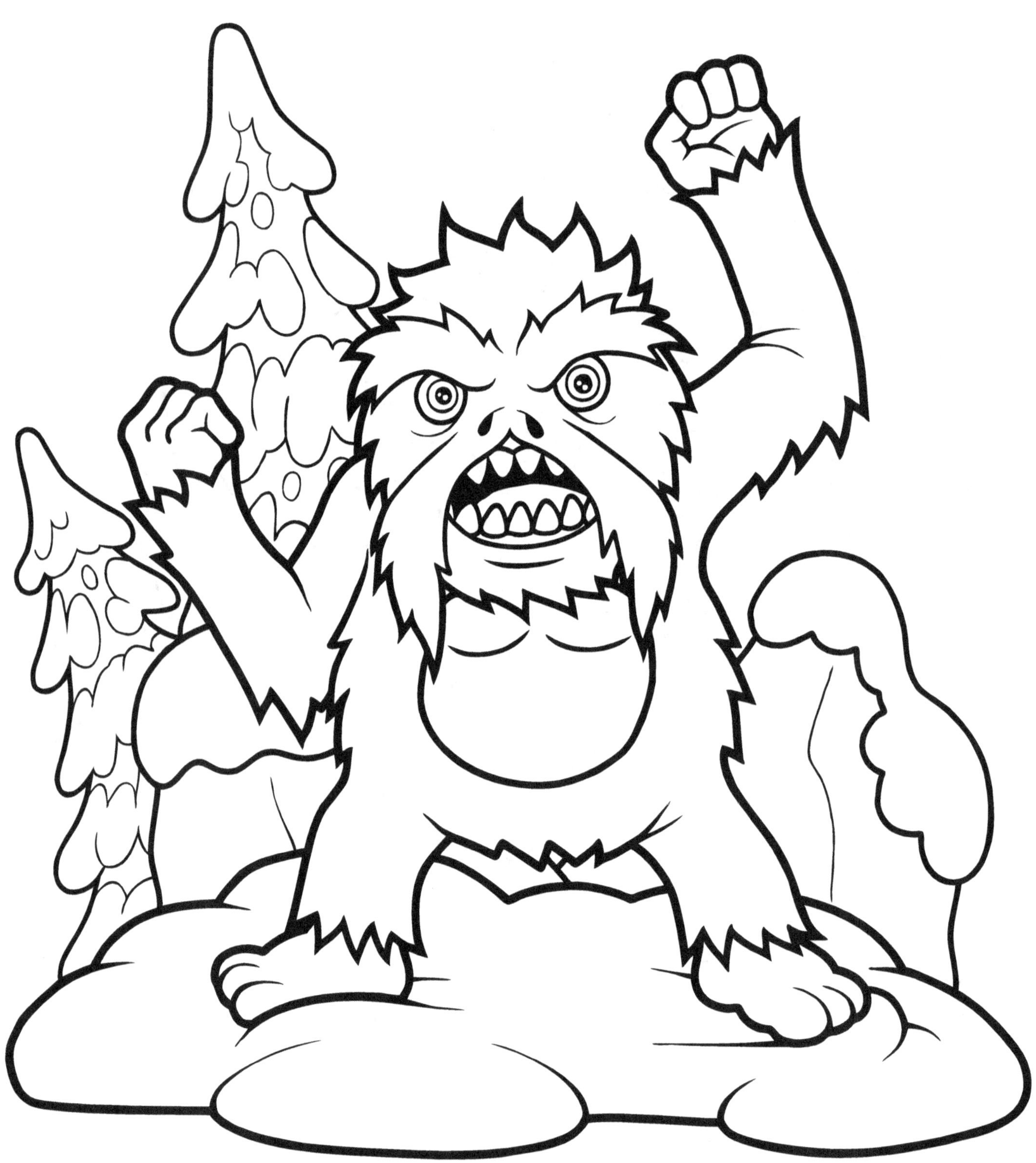

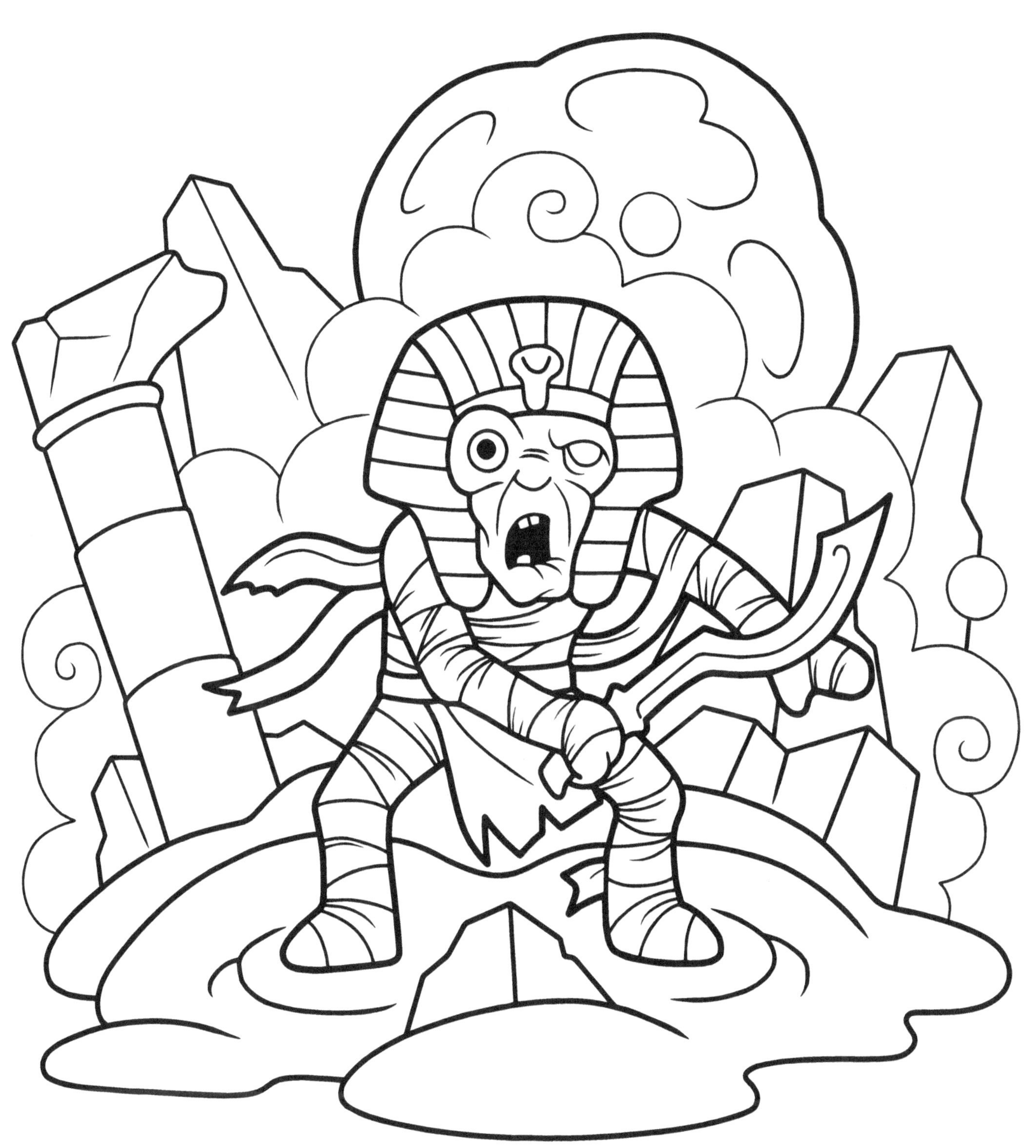

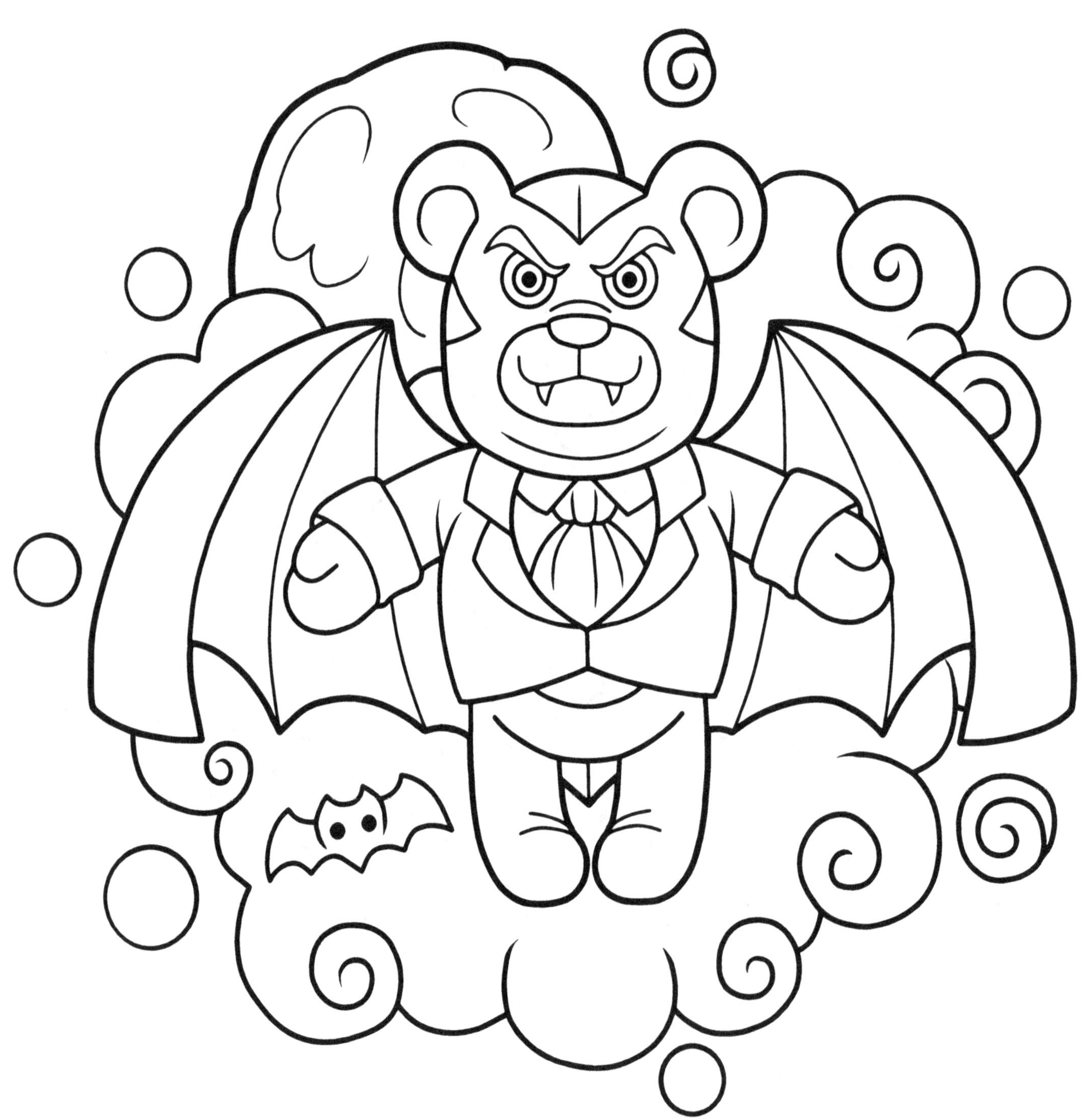

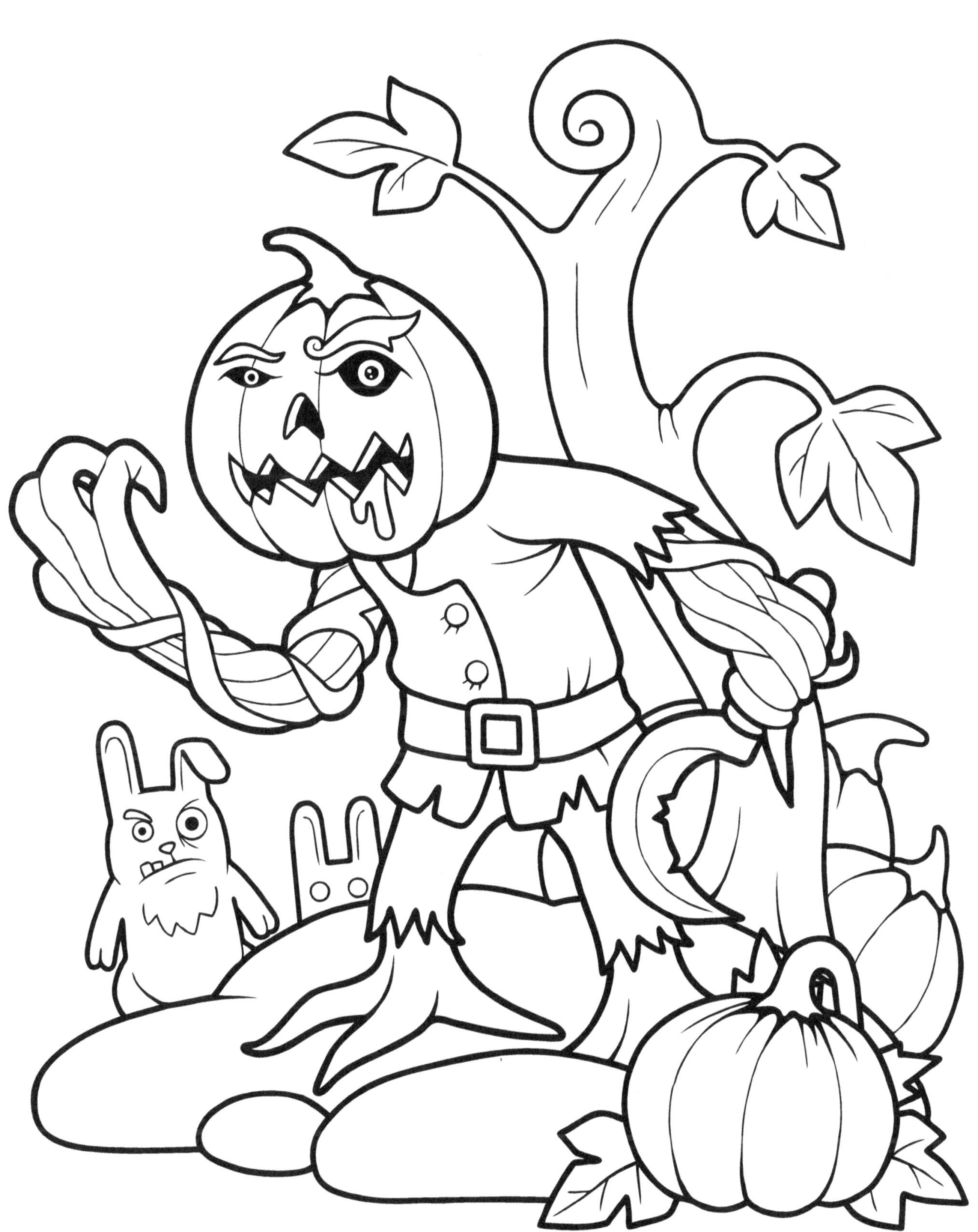

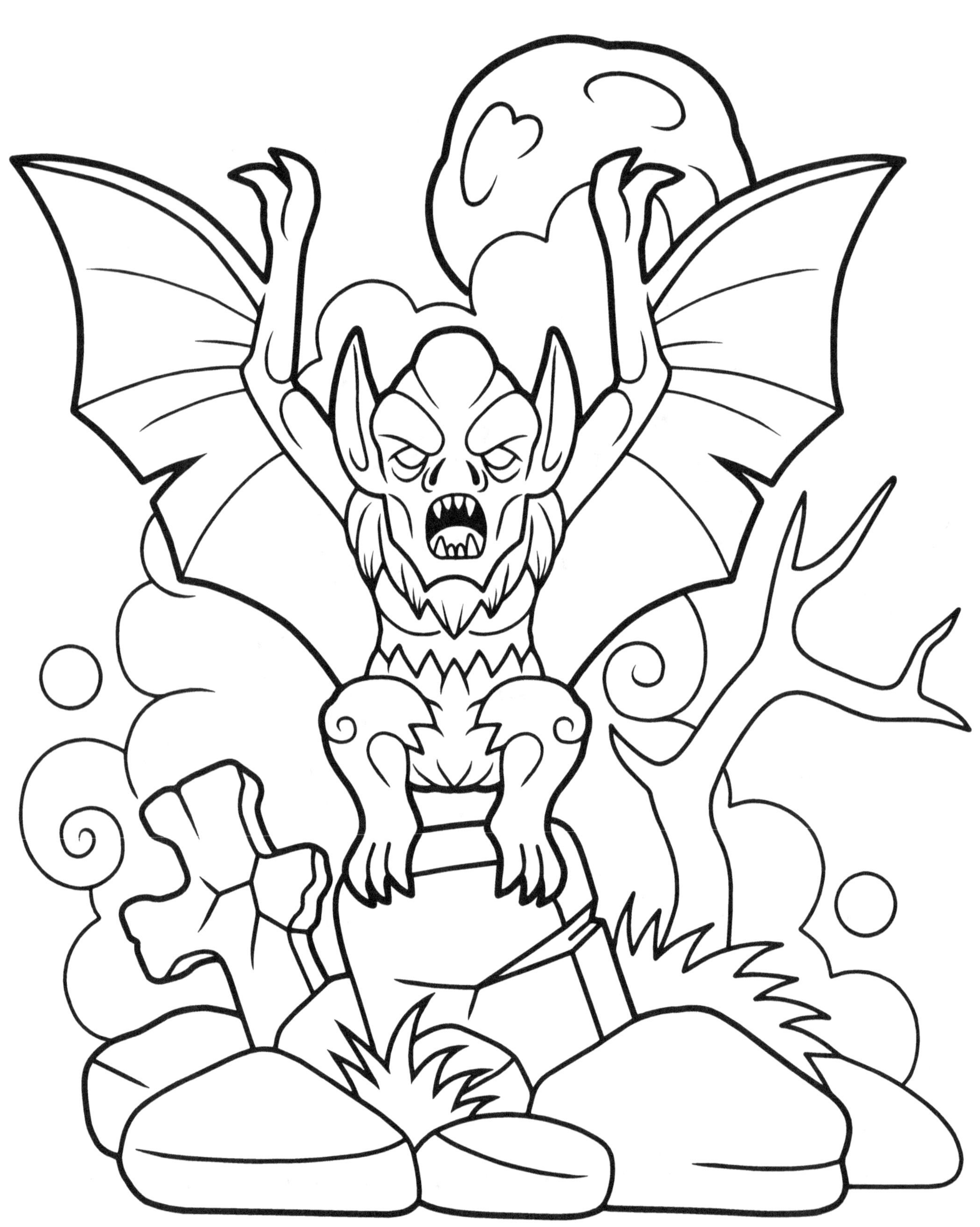

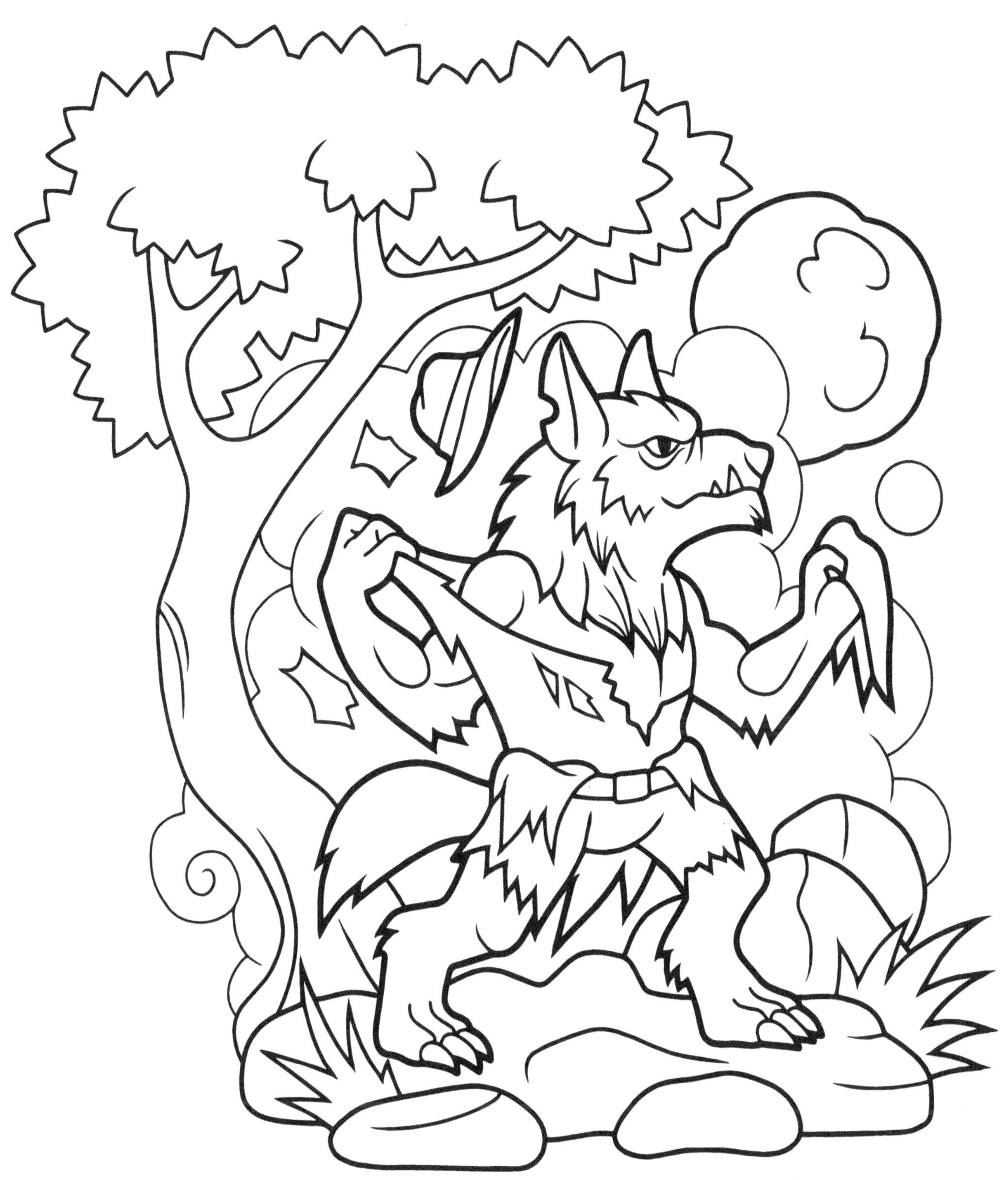

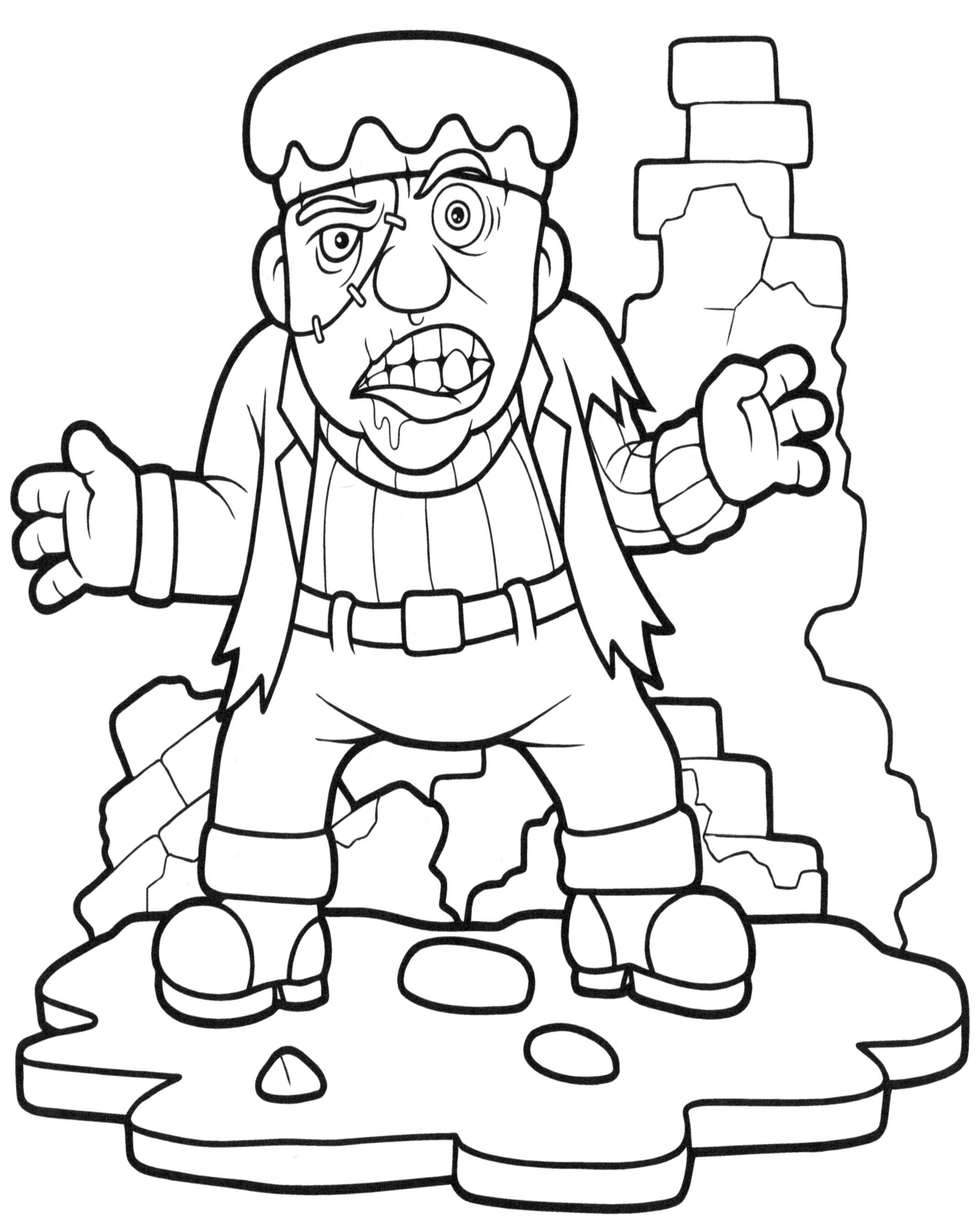

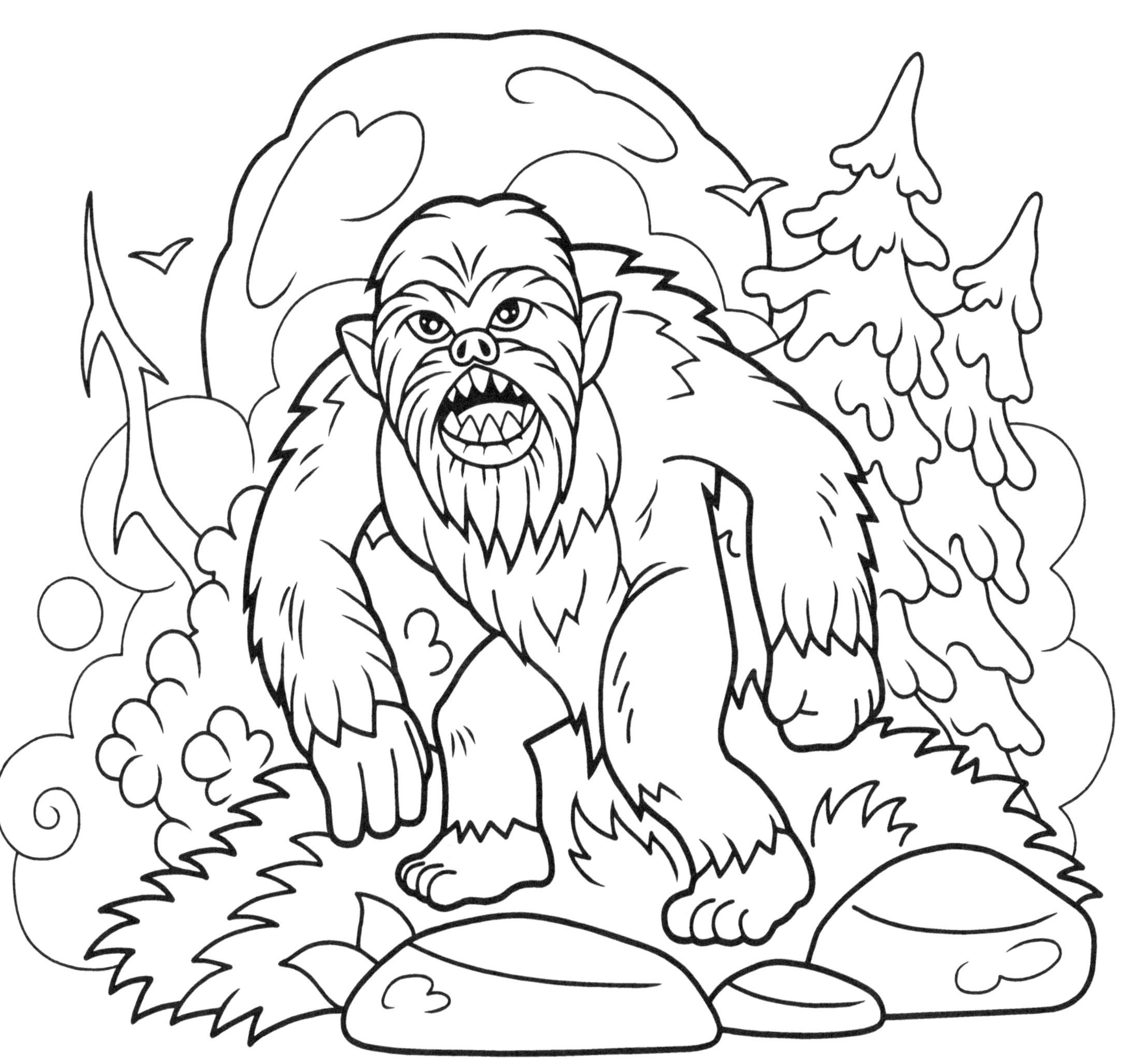

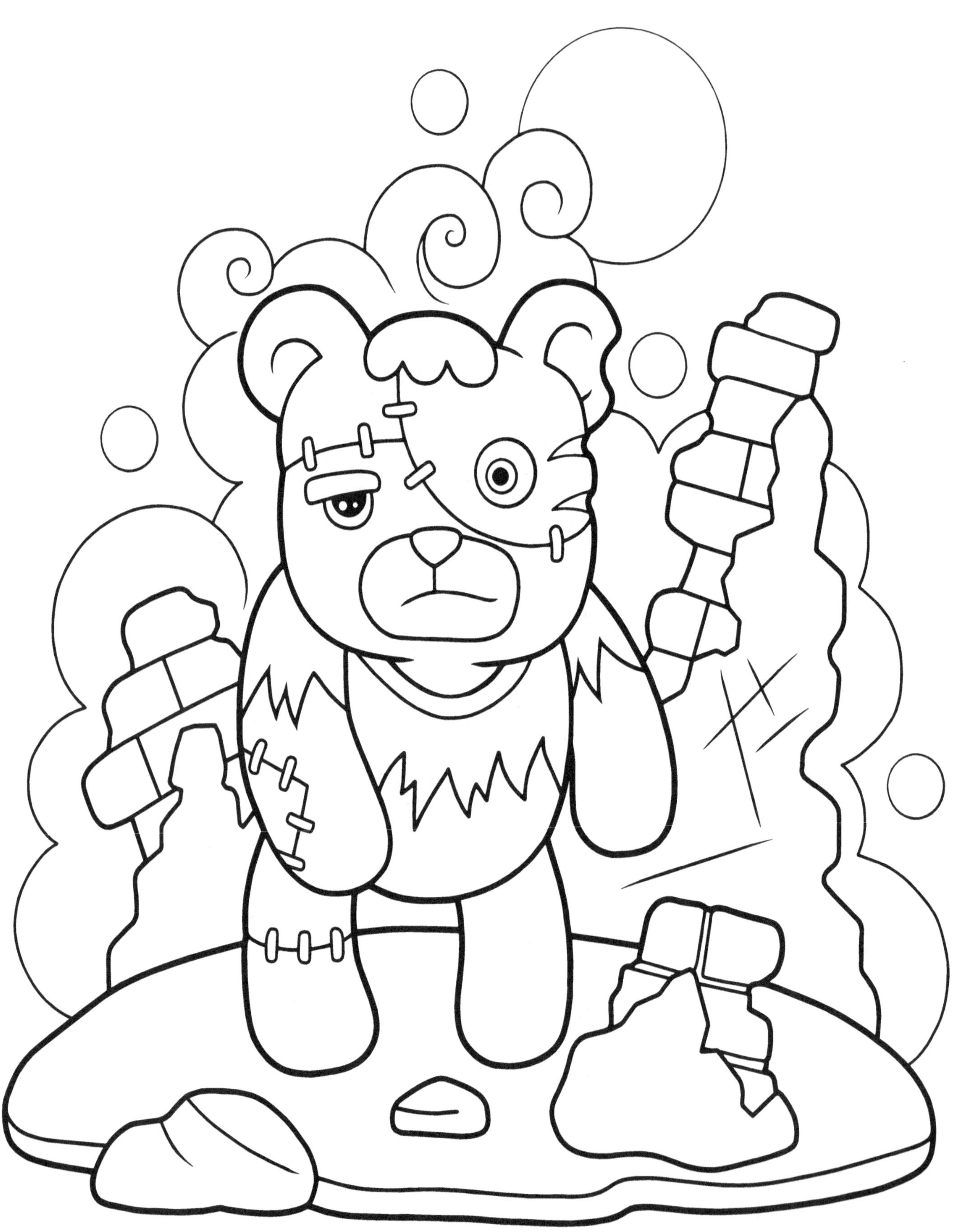

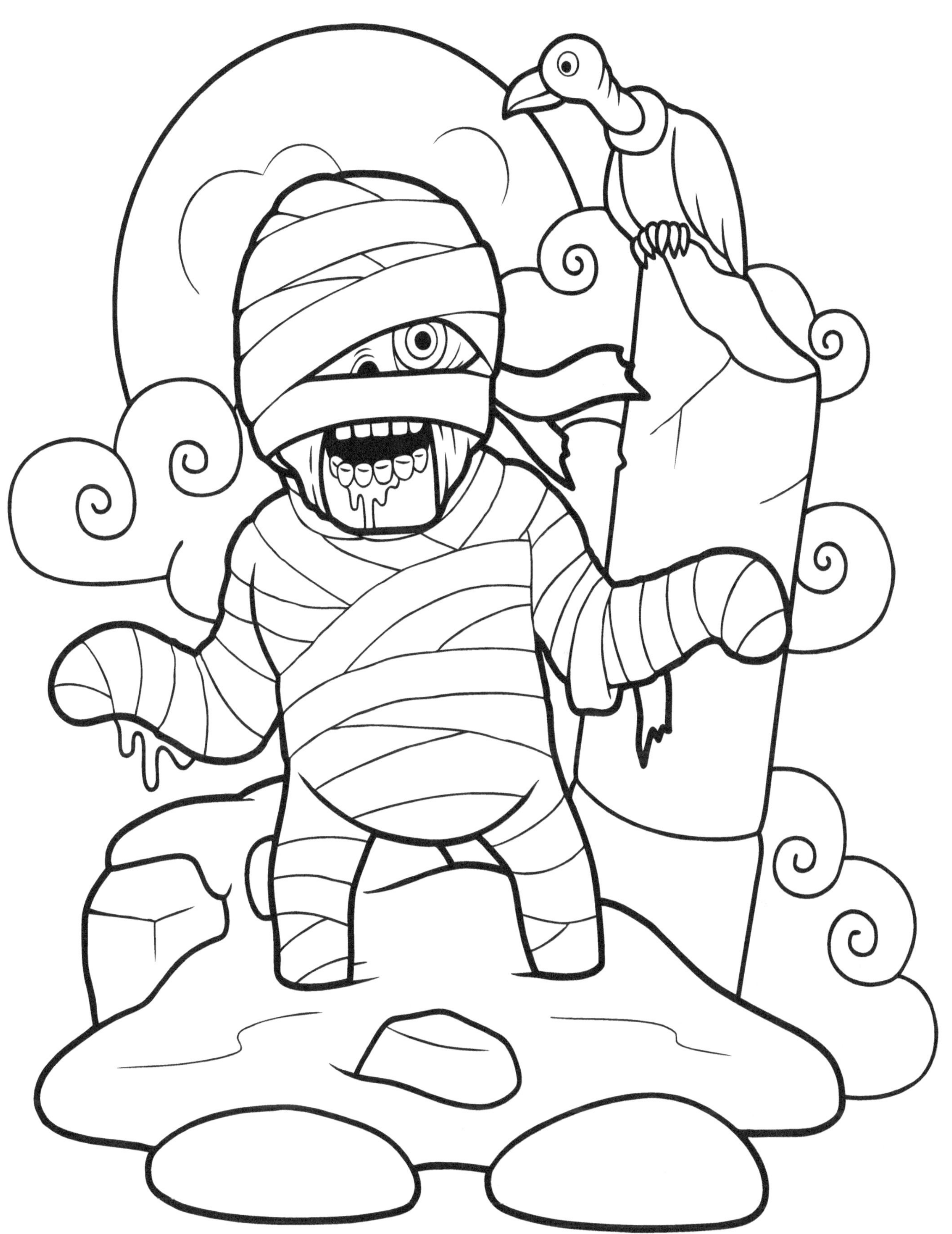

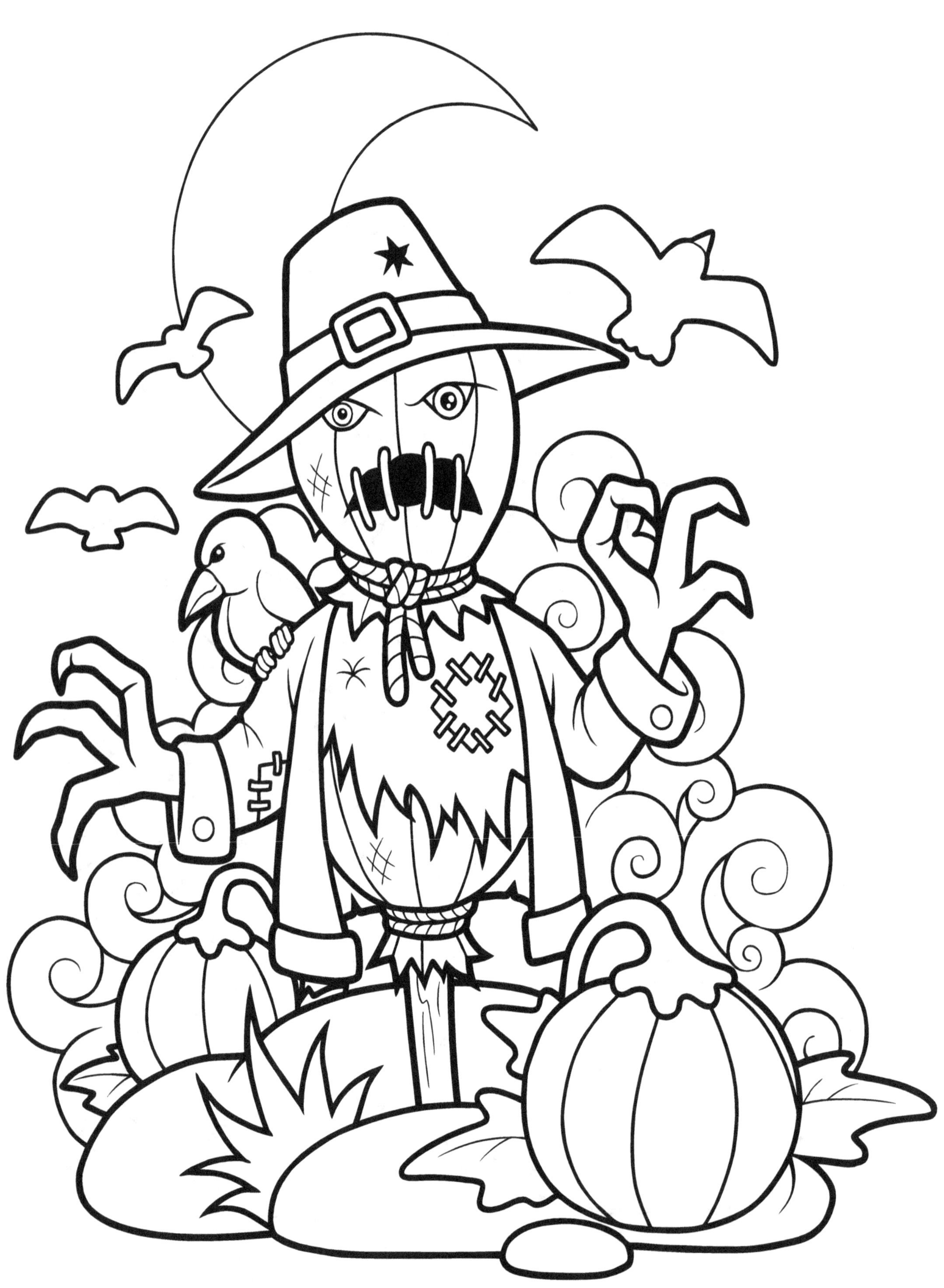

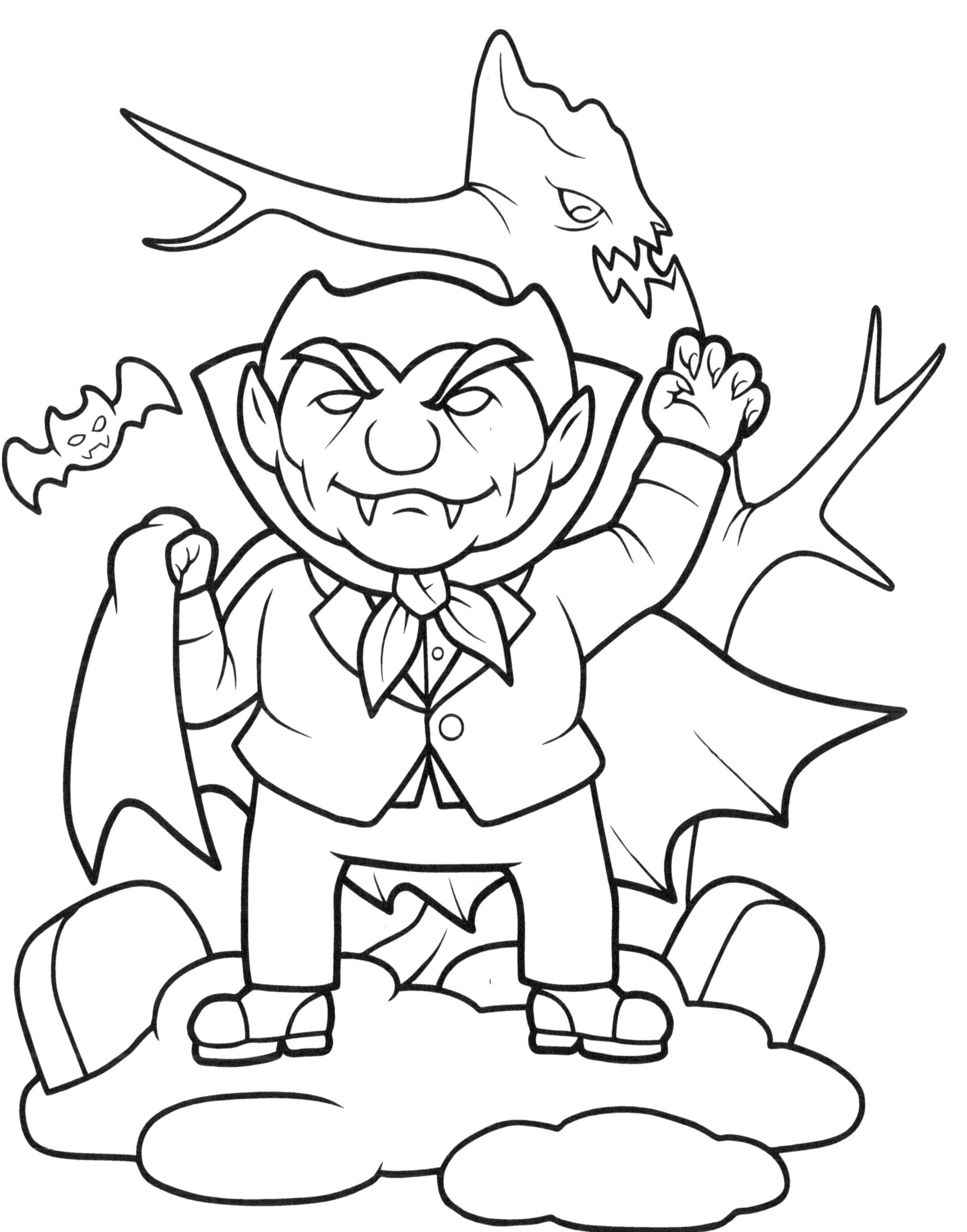

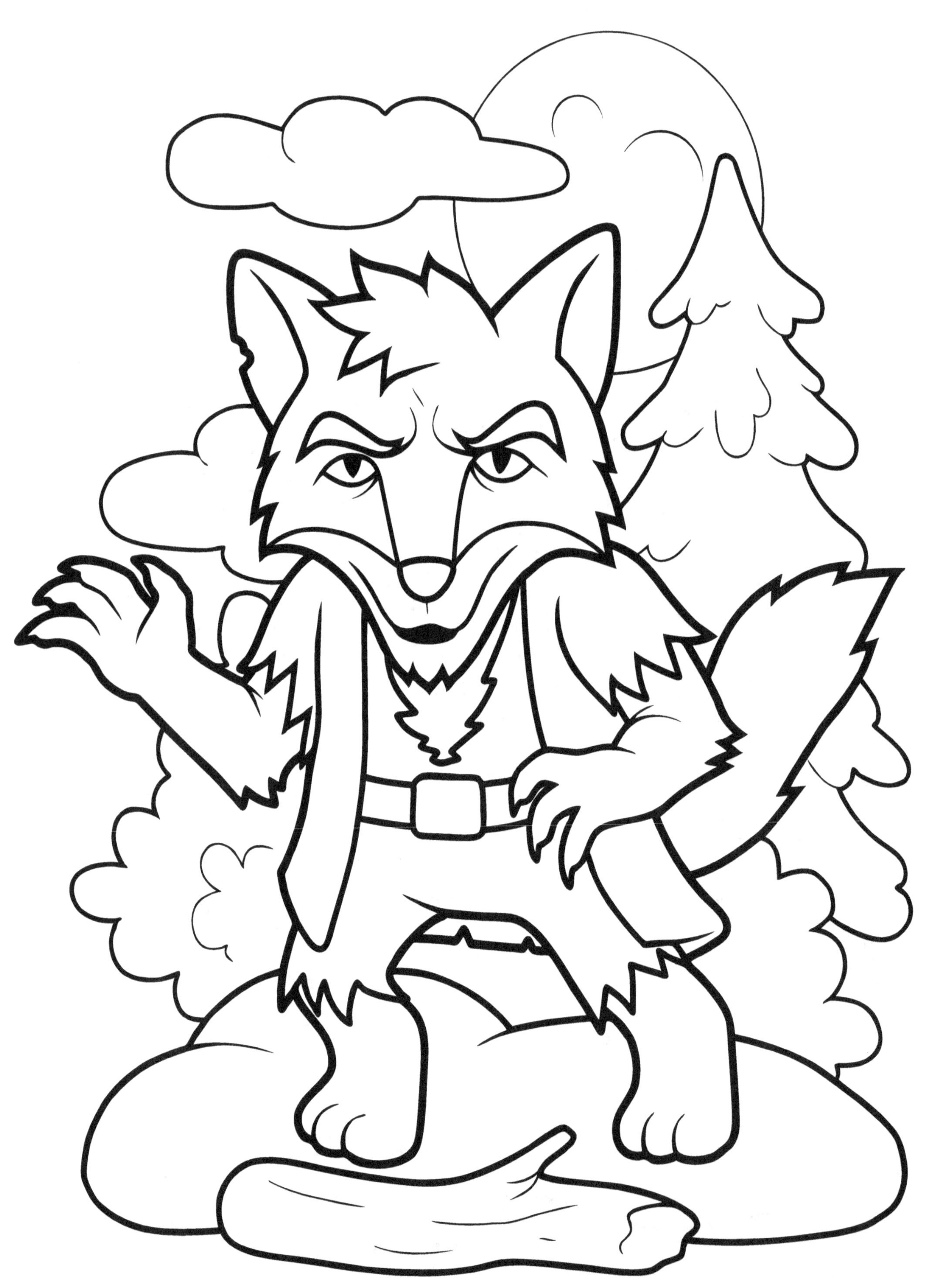

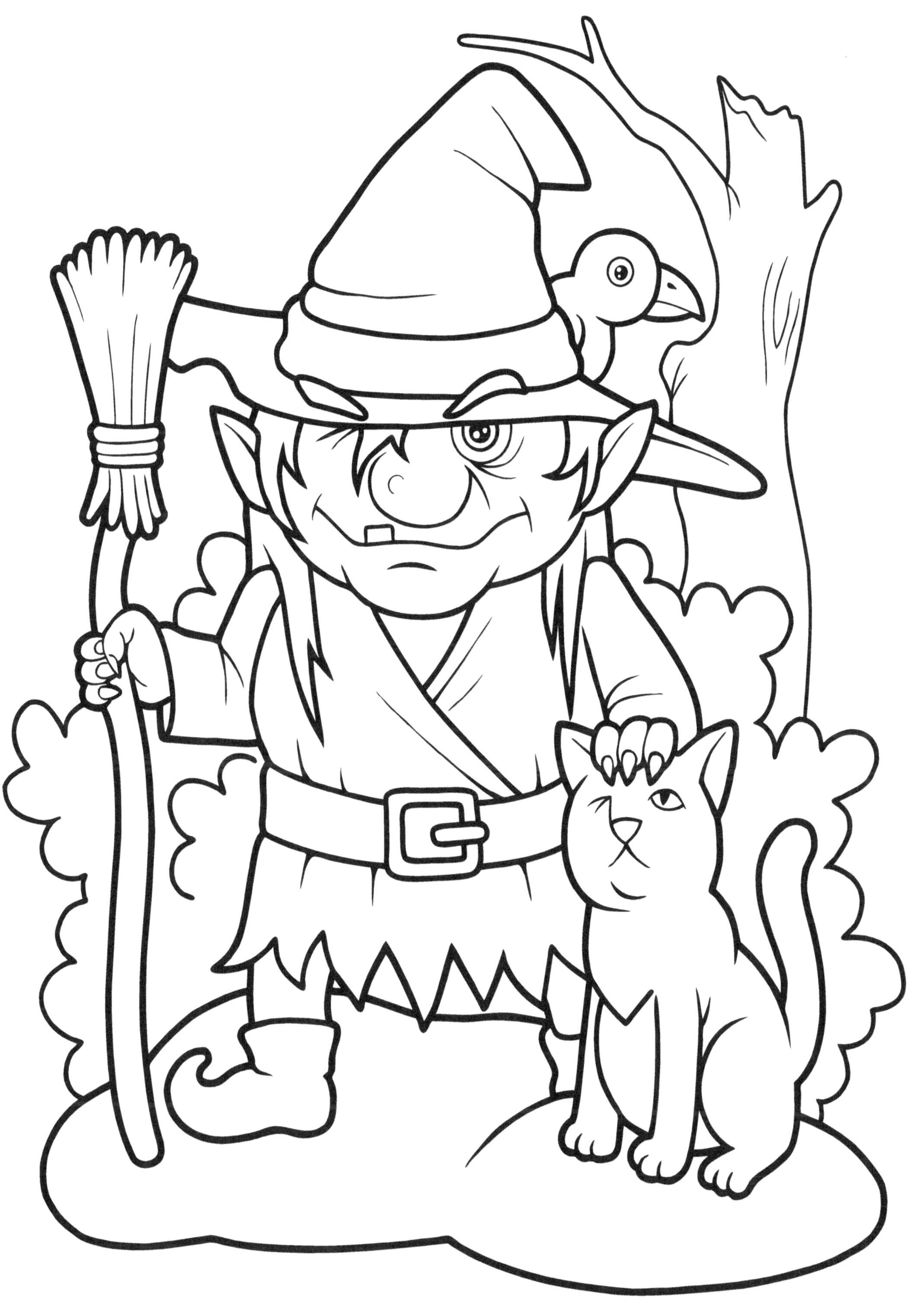

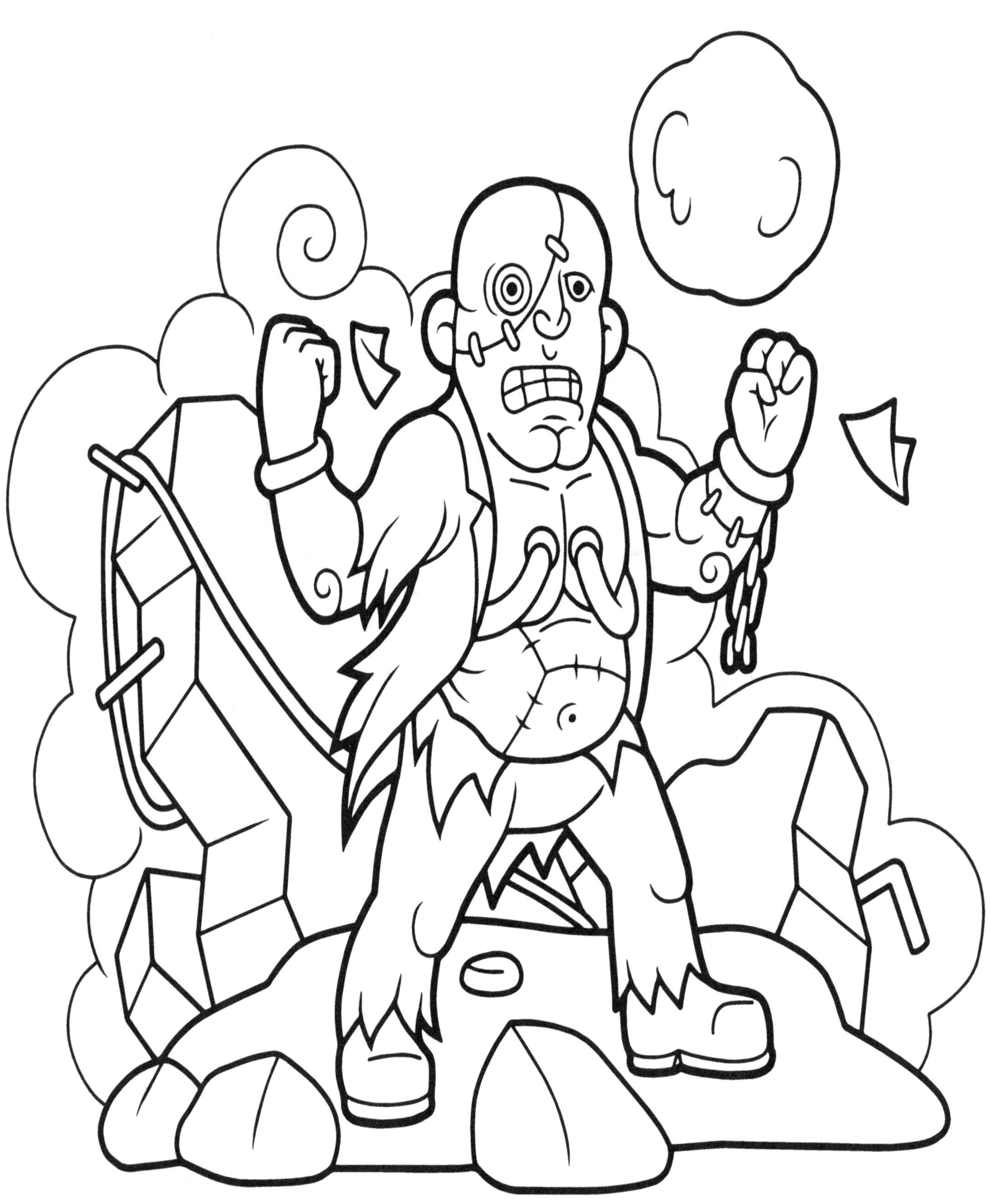

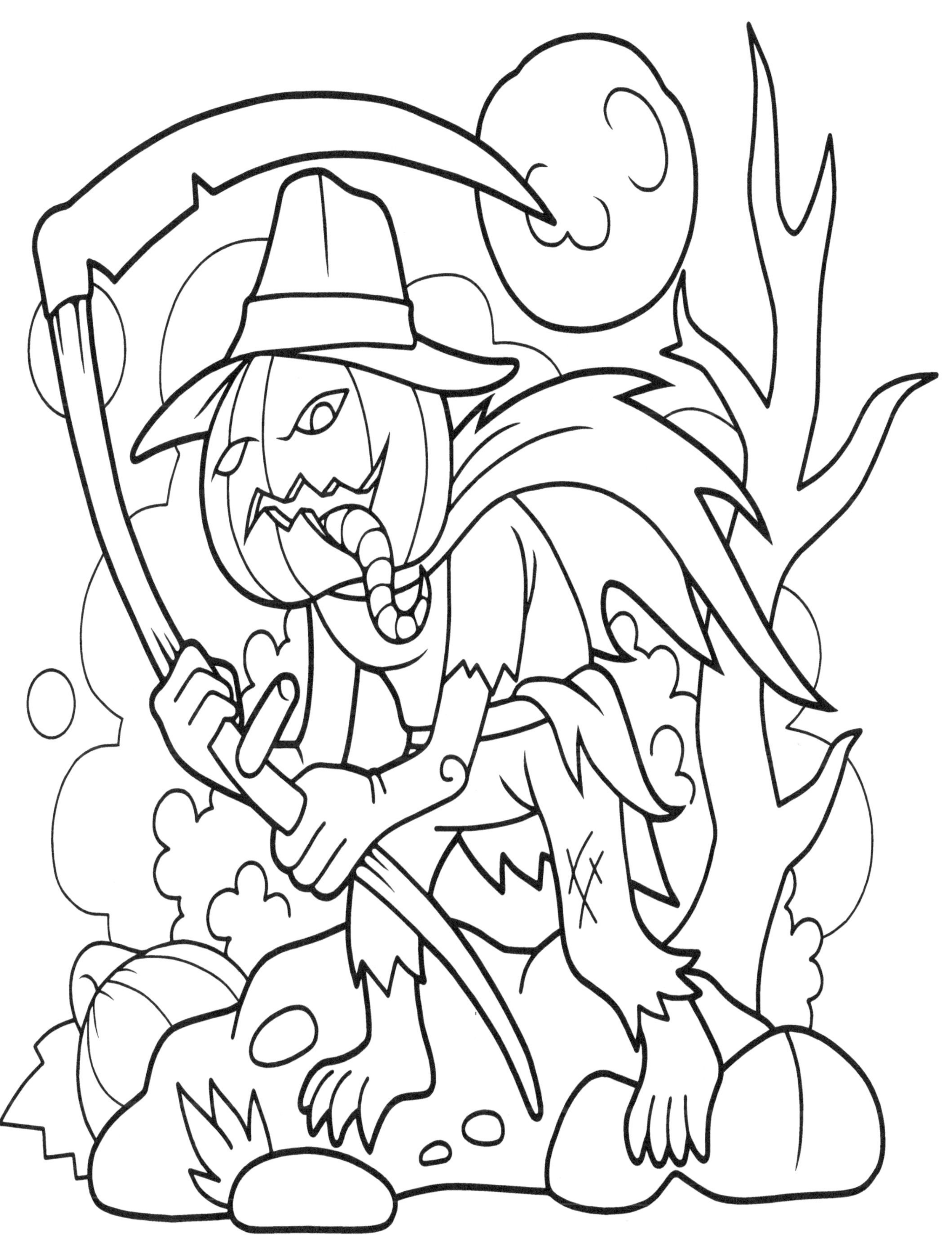

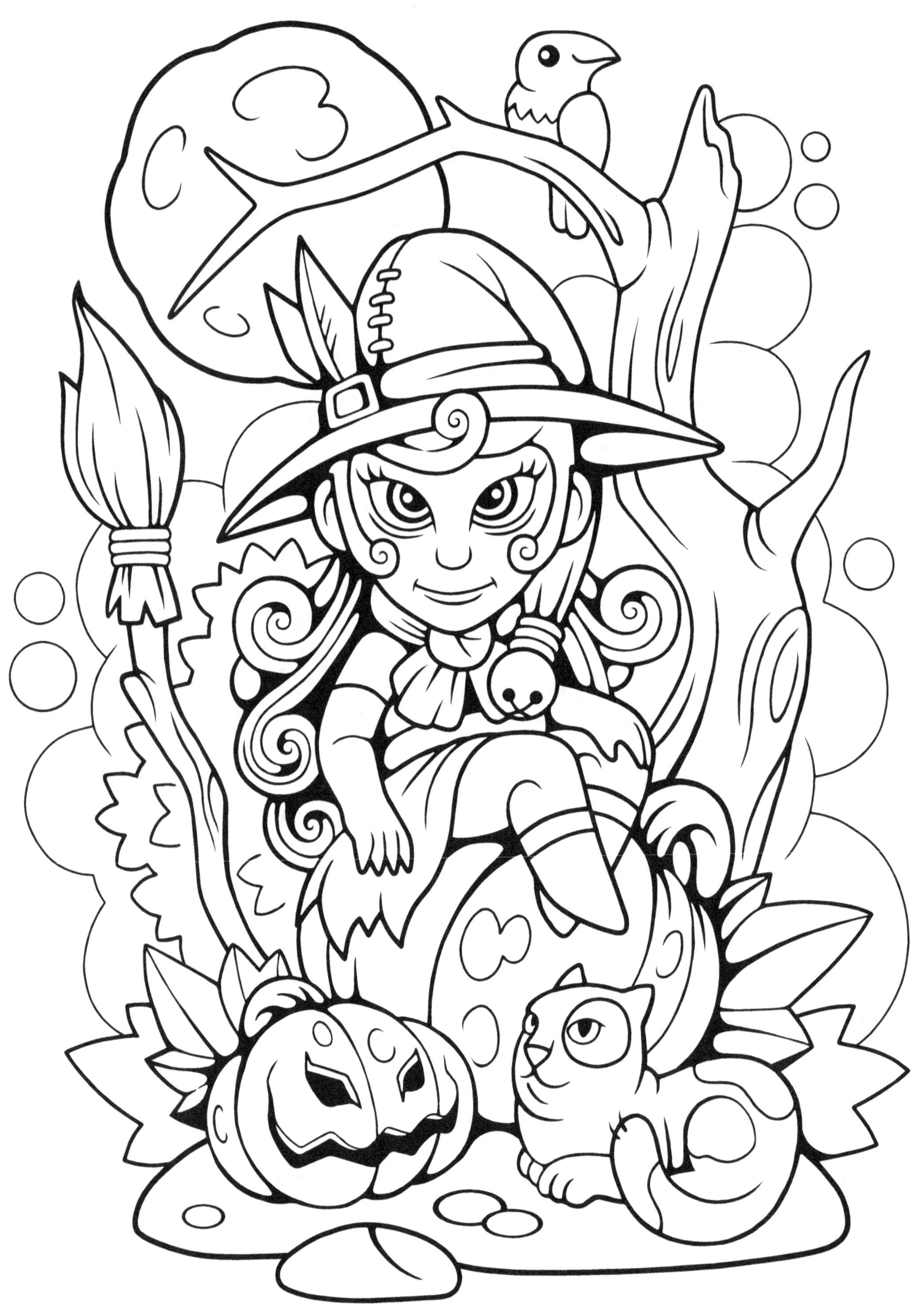

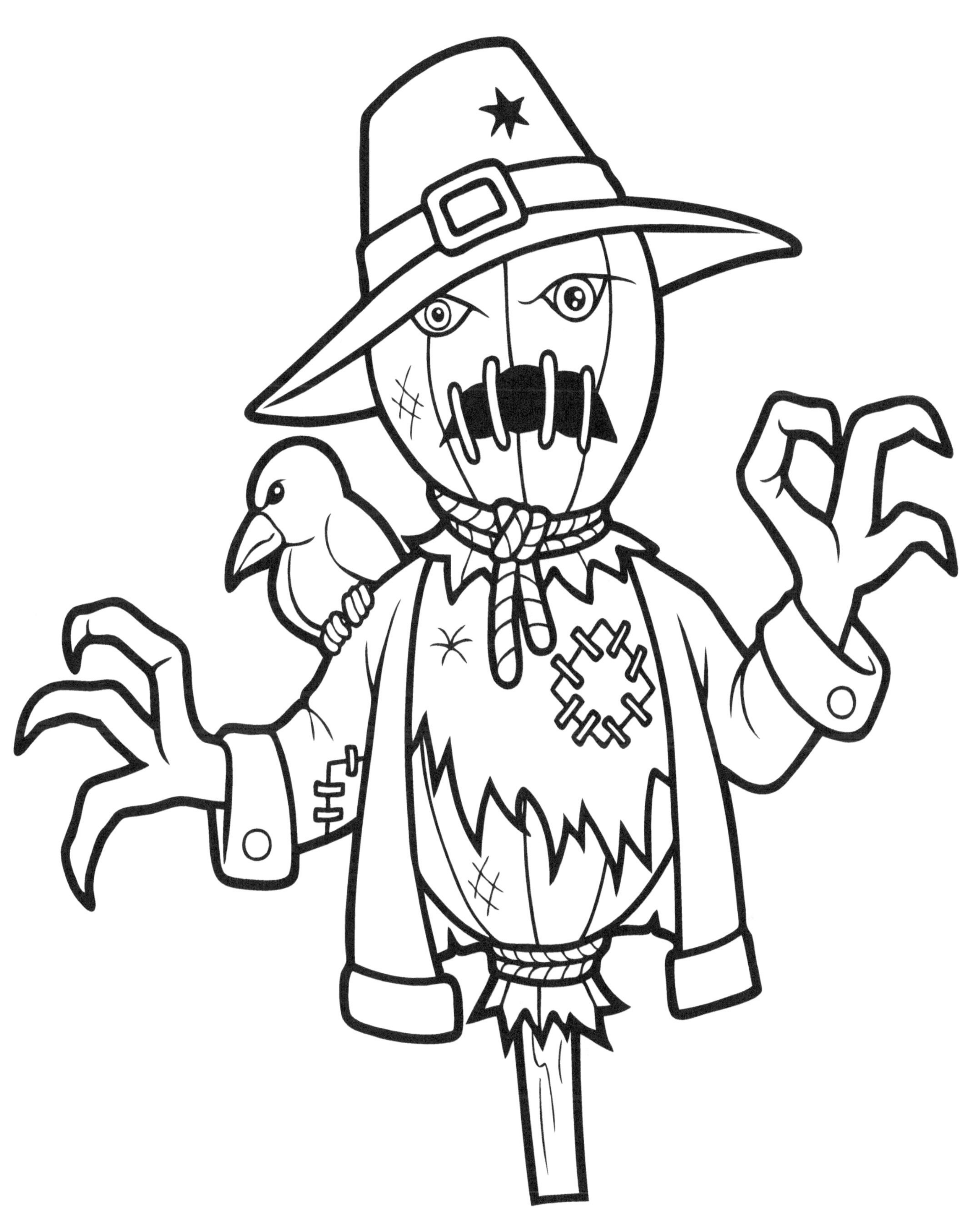

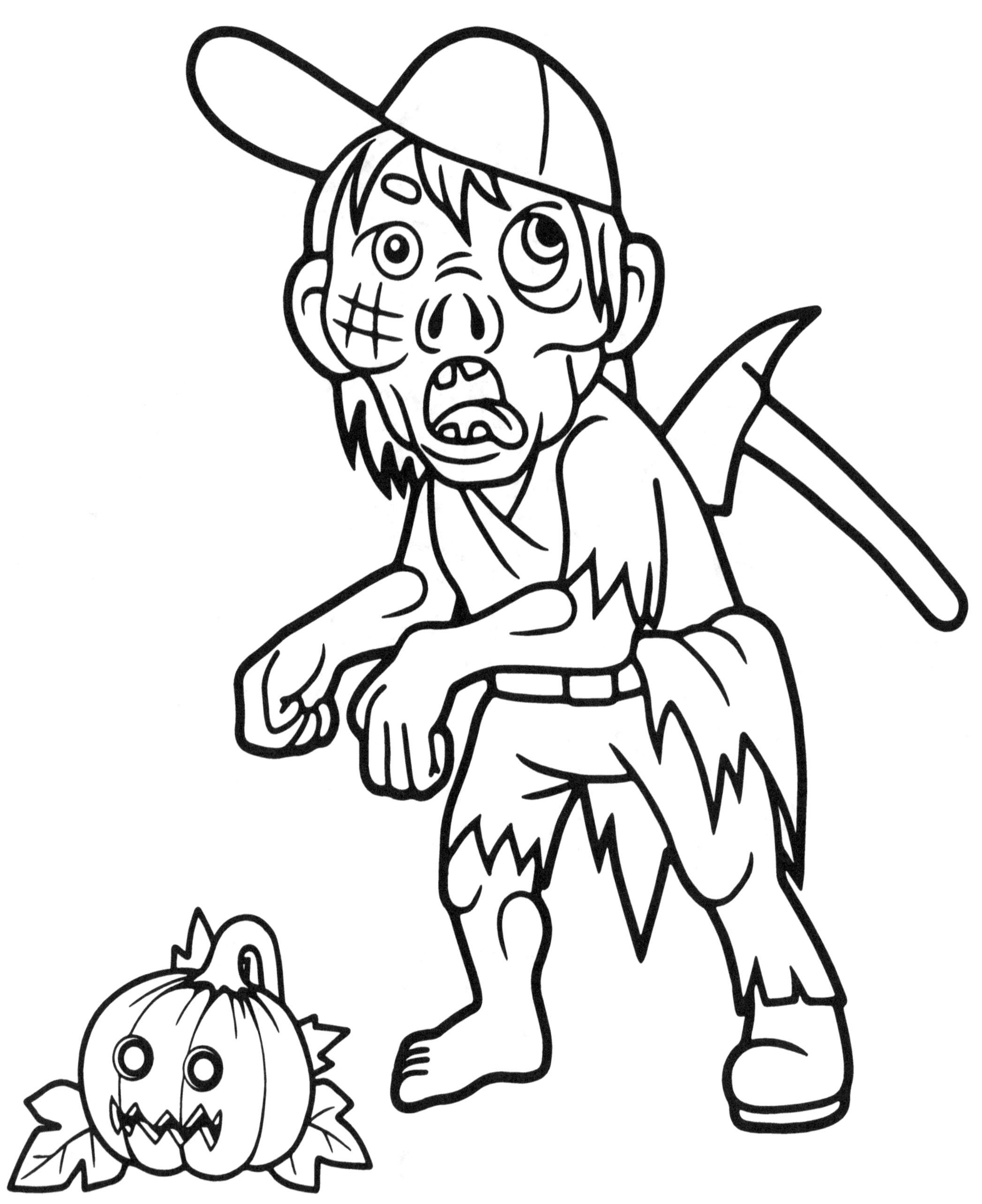

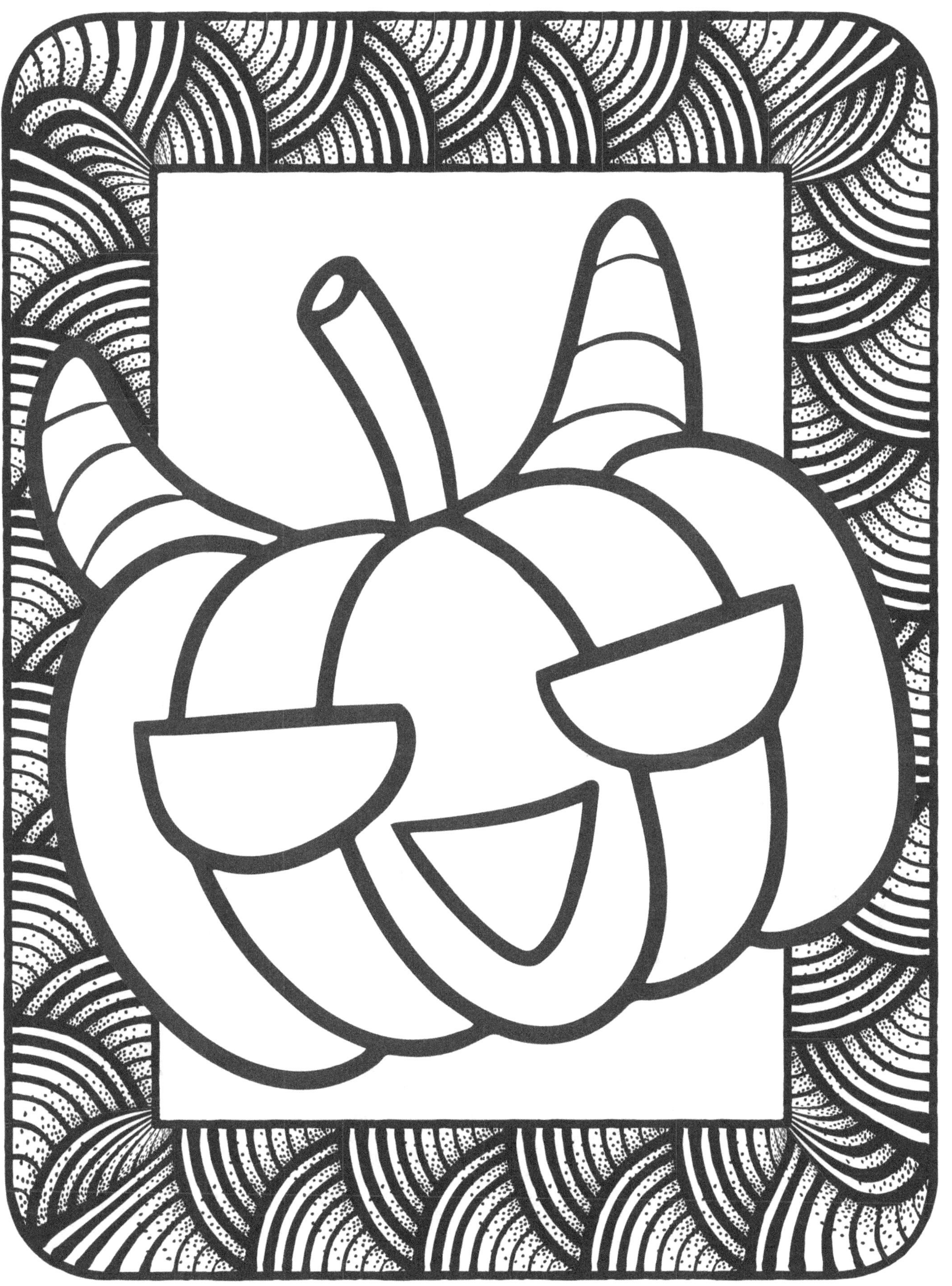

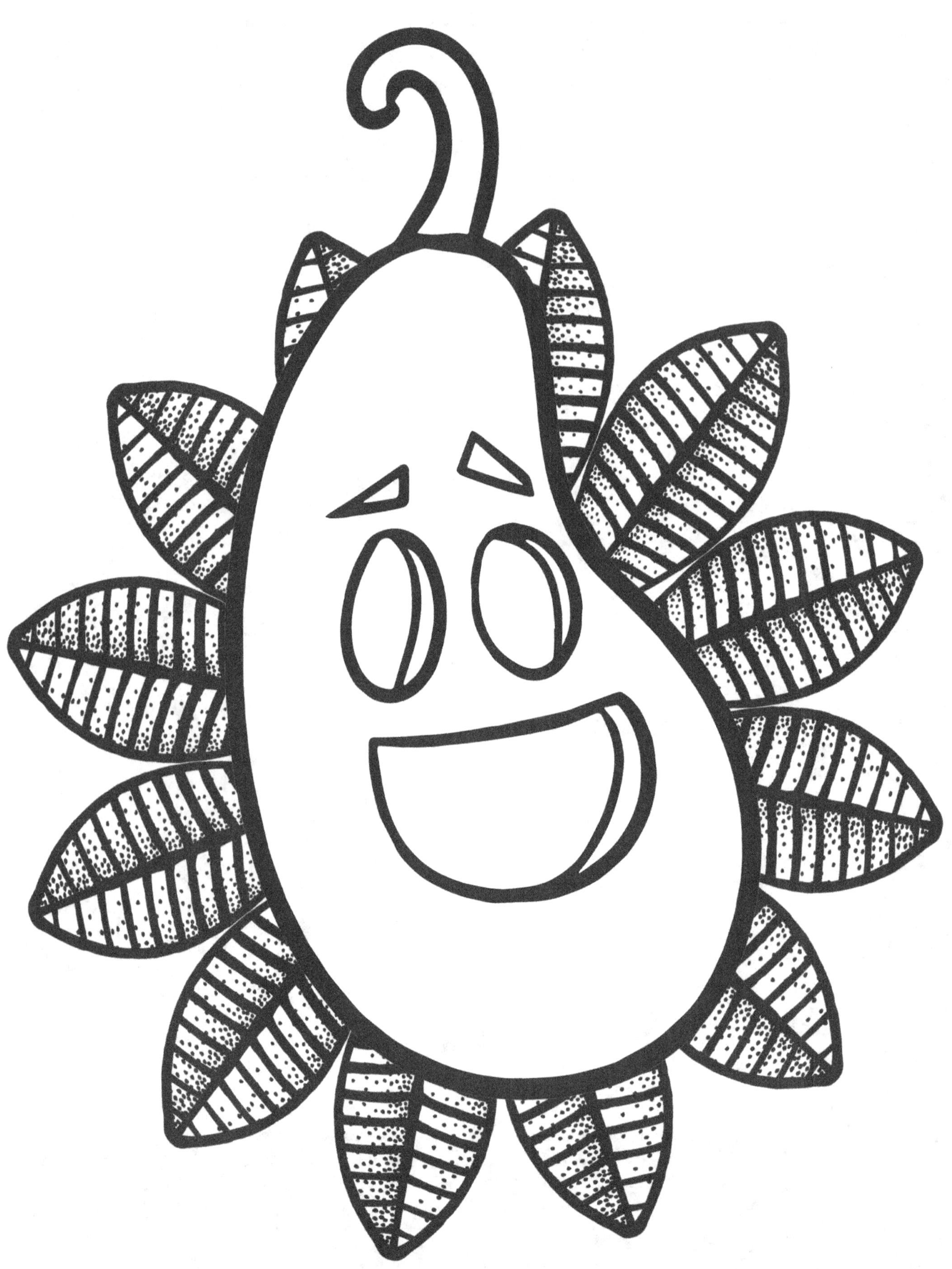

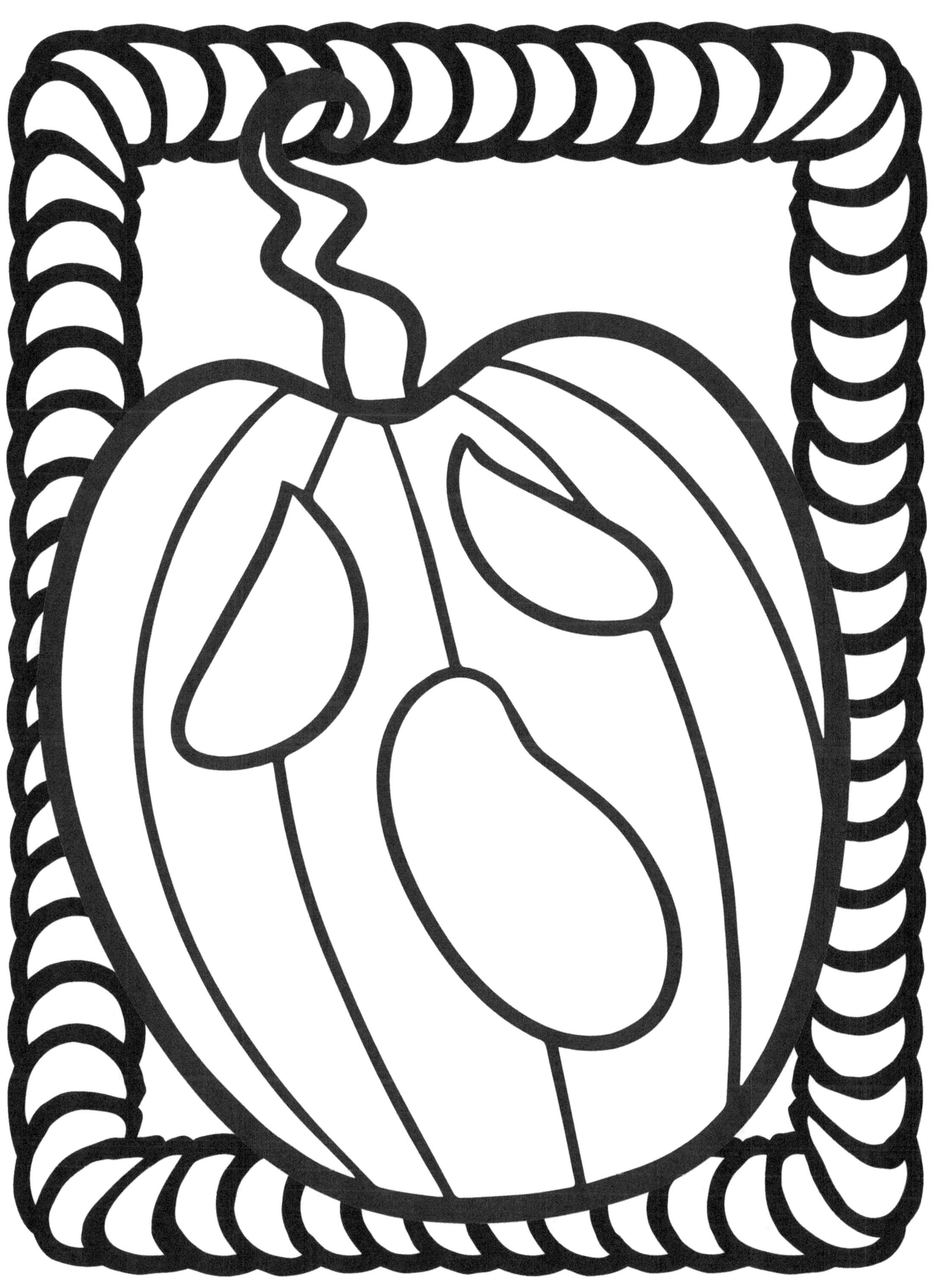

www.ingramcontent.com/pod-product-compliance
Lightning Source LLC
Chambersburg PA
CBHW080724120726
48001CB00010B/3139